Instructor Competencies

A volume in
The IBSTPI Book Series

The IBSTPI Book Series

Fieldbook of IBSTPI Evaluator Competencies (2014)
    Darlene F. Russ-Eft, Marcie J. Bober-Michel, Tiffany A. Koszalka, and Catherine M. Sleezer

Online Learner Competencies: Knowledge, Skills, and Attitudes for Successful Learning in Online Settings (2013)
    Michael Beaudoin, Gila Kurtz, Insung Jung, Katsuaki Suzuki, and Barbara L. Grabowski

Instructional Designer Competencies: The Standards (4th ed.; 2013)
    Tiffany A. Koszalka, Darlene F. Russ-Eft, and Robert Reiser

Instructor Competencies
The Standards, Fourth Edition

Kathy L. Jackson
The Pennsylvania State University

Florence Martin
North Carolina State University

Albert D. Ritzhaupt
University of Florida

INFORMATION AGE PUBLISHING, INC.
Charlotte, NC • www.infoagepub.com

Library of Congress Cataloging-in-Publication Data

A CIP record for this book is available from the Library of Congress
http://www.loc.gov

ISBN: 979-8-88730-401-4 (Paperback)
       979-8-88730-402-1 (Hardcover)
       979-8-88730-409-0 (E-Book)

Copyright © 2023 Information Age Publishing Inc.

All rights reserved. No part of this publication may be reproduced, stored in a retrieval system, or transmitted, in any form or by any means, electronic, mechanical, photocopying, microfilming, recording or otherwise, without written permission from the publisher.

Printed in the United States of America

CONTENTS

Foreword vii
James D. Klein

Preface.. ix
Fernando A. Senior Canela

1 Introduction: Instructor Competencies... 1

2 Instructor Competencies Development Model 23

3 Literature Review of Instructor Competencies................................. 39

4 Validation of Competencies.. 55

5 Core Instructor Competencies 69

6 Competencies for Blended Teaching 87

7 Competencies for Online Teaching 103

8 Instructor Competencies: Growth-Mindset Orientation
    and Continuous Development... 121

    Afterword 135

FOREWORD

The International Board of Standards for Training, Performance, and Instruction (IBSTPI) first published *Instructor Competencies: The Standards* in 1988. At that time, IBSTPI limited an instructor's role to the delivery of instruction. They were responsible for supporting learning in face-to-face settings by delivering content, making demonstrations, facilitating discussions, and administering assessments. Then in 2004, IBSTPI published *Instructor Competencies: Standards for Face-to-Face, Online, and Blended Settings* in recognition that instruction was no longer constrained by time and place. The 2004 IBSTPI competencies reflected developments in the strategies, tools, and settings available to instructors due to emerging technologies and an emphasis on learner-centered instruction.

Over the past 20 years, we have continued to witness changes to how we view teaching and learning. Instructors communicate and interact with learners using new technology tools. They curate online content that learners can access asynchronously. Instructors use learning management systems to develop and implement instruction and they use learning analytics to evaluate learners' progress. Instructors create and participate in communities of practice and facilitate learning through gamification, microlearning, flipped classrooms, and virtual reality.

What has not changed is IBSTPI's mission to develop, validate, and promote the implementation of international standards to advance training,

Instructor Competencies, pages vii–viii
Copyright © 2023 by Information Age Publishing
www.infoagepub.com
All rights of reproduction in any form reserved.

instruction, learning, and performance improvement of individuals and organizations. The updated instructor competencies presented in this book reflect current theory, research, and practice on learning and instruction. They are organized under four domains (foundational, design, facilitation, and evaluation) and include 19 competencies and 150 evidence-based performance statements validated by over 500 survey respondents.

As a former board member and someone who uses competencies in my research and practice, I am delighted that IBSTPI has updated the instructor competencies. I encourage readers to reflect on their own practice to determine how it can be improved by implementing IBSTPI's work.

—**James D. Klein**
Florida State University

PREFACE

What makes someone exceptionally good at what they do? Having attempted to answer the previous question, how do you conduct an international study to validate your description of expert behavior and later share your results with the world, hoping it becomes an aspirational benchmark of professional excellence?

Welcome to the essential mission of the International Board of Standards for Training, Performance, and Instruction. For over 46 years, several generations of passionate *pro bono* researchers and practitioners have pondered, discussed, analyzed, researched, written, and promoted professional competencies in the learning field.

WHY IS THIS BOOK UNIQUE?

The book you are holding is a masterpiece, like a pinecone of a sequoia tree. A single pinecone of these millennial trees contains an average of two hundred seeds carrying the DNA of the oldest-known living trees on the planet, roughly 3,000 years old. Similarly, in less than 160 pages, this book contains the historical legacy of an organization that has studied the competencies of instructors for 35 years, a considerable length of time when you factor in the impact of technology on human behavior. Consider that the first edition of instructor competencies was published in 1988, 1 year before Sir Tim Berners-Lee, a British scientist, invented the World Wide Web (WWW) while working at the European Organization of Research (CERN).

Instructor Competencies, pages ix–xii
Copyright © 2023 by Information Age Publishing
www.infoagepub.com
All rights of reproduction in any form reserved.

WHO IS THIS BOOK FOR, AND HOW TO USE IT?

Regardless of their context and job titles, instructors—from elementary education teachers to university faculty to trainers in corporate settings or armed forces, or virtual facilitators in non-profit organizations—will find valuable insights from the breadth and depth of the revised competencies and performance statements. Administrators and policymakers may benefit from a contemporary portrayal of the nuances of the teaching or facilitation modalities and their administrative, legal, technological, and logistical considerations. The book contains intriguing questions that beg for further probing and will most likely germinate like seeds in a field of new research studies. Many studies, including doctoral dissertations, have already used the IBSTPI competencies as a benchmark for subsequent research. The inclusion of recent research citations facilitates the work of future research.

ABOUT THE REFINEMENT OF THE RESEARCH METHODS AND ANALYSIS

This book contains more hidden treasures that may be less apparent to the newly initiated IBSTPI follower: The special attention placed on the evolution of today's teaching modalities and the sophistication of the data analysis. While IBSTPI competencies have been intentionally technology-neutral, instructors' working conditions changed radically with the normalization of face-to-face, hybrid, and fully online modalities. Hence, the new competencies adopted these distinctions for the first time. Likewise, recent neuroscience research also led to integrating a new lens to address the concept of a growth mindset and its impact on performance. Finally, unlike any previous validation studies, the data analysis was considerably more meticulous in parceling out differences in the demographic characteristics of the instructor competencies survey participants, such as gender, geographic location, educational level, and face-to-face teaching experience.

In the era of instant query on the Internet, including generative text algorithms, when one could obtain instant recommendations of "required competencies" for instructors or other professions, it is reassuring to find descriptions of competent behavior resulting from systematic research, expert deliberations, and academic craftsmanship.

Congratulations to the team for sustaining an exceptionally long process to bring a revised set of instructor competencies to life, maintaining and expanding the research-based tradition of IBSTPI.

ACKNOWLEDGMENTS

It is important to recognize that this internationally conducted study, along with this book, required the contributions of many individuals across a range of diverse settings. The ongoing support provided by the various IBSTPI boards of directors who served during the design and data collection of the instructor competencies study was instrumental to the success of this process. In particular, several individuals contributed significant effort and contributions to the design and development of the study and to the writing of this book.

When IBSTPI conducts a revision or develops a new set of competencies, a small group of people are tasked with a needs assessment to ascertain next steps and then, if deemed appropriate, they use the IBSTPI competency model to identify and validate competencies. We owe many thanks to the dedicated efforts of Tiffany A. Koszalka (Syracuse University), Barbara Grabowski (Emerita, Penn State University), Ileana de la Teja (Open University of Catalunya), and Kathy L. Jackson (Penn State University), who thoroughly conducted a revision and update of the instructor competencies and readied them for internal and external reviews before labeling them ready for the next step in the process. Chapter 2 of this book details their process and results.

With the new competencies deemed ready for the validation study, it was decided that a robust, enhanced survey tool was needed to enable block-based questionnaire design and logical branching options. The new instructor competencies contain 157 performance statements within 19 competencies organized into four domains, and the design and development of the questionnaire was skillfully done by Abdulrahman Alogaily (King Saud University).

IBSTPI board members, former IBSTPI affiliates, and professional organizations (e.g., AECT) were instrumental in promoting and distributing the questionnaire internationally. In addition to thanking those who facilitated our reaching a broad and distributed group of study participants, we want to recognize and thank the 578 who responded to the questionnaire. The depth and quality of these responses made this study not only possible, but powerful.

In addition to the writing team of Kathy L. Jackson (Penn State University), Florence Martin (North Carolina State University), and Albert D. Ritzhaupt (University of Florida), we want to acknowledge the contributions of Andrew Stricker (Air University). Without his vision, our competency definition would not include the timely and needed "growth identity." With his guidance, we were motivated to include a Chapter 8 that situates the growth identity and its relevance in today's teaching and learning competencies.

The work of IBSTPI continues because of its connections to a committed group of scholars, students, researchers, learning and instructional specialists in many contexts, and others. We appreciate all of you who helped make this work possible. Thank you.

— **Fernando A Senior Canela, PhD**
Digital Learning Strategist
IBSTPI Fellow and Past President
Quality Matters representative for Latin America
and the Caribbean

CHAPTER 1

INTRODUCTION

Instructor Competencies

OVERVIEW

In this book, we present an updated and revised set of instructor competencies based on the International Board of Standards for Training, Performance, and Instruction (IBSTPI) 2004 set of instructor competencies. Today's 21st-century instructional skills still contain foundational skills that are applicable in most settings and with most target learners, but technology and adaptability to it is becoming an expectation. This book, the fourth iteration of IBSTPI's instructor competencies, leverages current pedagogical evidence-based findings into the new competencies and reflects today's dynamic instructional contexts. This first chapter introduces instructor competencies by first defining some key terms and providing IBSTPI's perspective on these terms, describes why we updated and validated a new set of instructor competencies, and provides an overview of key trends in today's instructional landscapes.

Orienting Questions

- Who is an instructor?
- What does it mean to be competent?

> - Can we identify competent instructors?
> - How has IBSTPI contributed to the field of instructor competencies?
> - How do advances in evidence-based instruction and instructional technologies impact instructor competencies?
> - What is the relationship between an instructor's role(s) and learning modality?

INSTRUCTOR COMPETENCY FUNDAMENTALS

With any area of study, terminology and a common understanding of its use are needed. For example, using the terms *teacher* and *instructor* interchangeably suggests that these important roles in instructional settings are viewed as the same. If we look at the definition of a teacher—"A person who teaches, especially in a school"—and then look at the definition of an instructor—"A person who teaches something"—it is hard to make much of a distinction. It is when we look at the different roles, rank, and levels of those who teach, however, that we can more clearly differentiate. While international differences in the use of these terms may exist, in looking at the United States' use of these terms, we find that teachers are educators who work with students in primary and secondary settings. The terms professor, instructor, and lecturer designate those teaching primarily in higher education or in informal education settings. In this book, "instructor" is used because it is synonymous with numerous types of educators including, for example, trainers, professors, mentors, or tutors.

We also make a distinction between a student and a learner. A student needs a teacher, and a learner is someone seeking knowledge or a skill with or without a teacher. *The Glossary of Education Reform* (2014) elaborates:

> While this preference may seem arbitrary on the surface, it does appear to serve a semantic purpose: learning can occur in the absence of teaching, but teaching doesn't occur without some form of learning taking place. I.e., learners can learn without teachers, but students are only students when they have teachers. (para. 2)

Our intentional selection of the term learner highlights the importance of individuals who bring knowledge and a willingness to learn to instructional settings. Of significance is a broader concept of learner to include instructors as active participants in learning.

How do we know if an instructor is effective? Teaching effectiveness is hard to define, given that teaching is multilayered and complex. We can, however, identify the knowledge, skills, and abilities that are the competencies enabling an instructor to be effective. We also recognize that instruction is a complex process and requires more than subject knowledge and know-how; a pedagogical skill set and an ability to connect with learners are also needed. Although teaching effectiveness is not commonly understood, it is generally recognized as "the effects of teaching on student learning" (Seidel & Shaverson, 2007, p. 454). Moreover, "effective teaching is a hypothetical construct for which there is no single indicator" (Marsh et al., 2011, p. 735) and yet, despite the multilayered complexity to instructing, there are assumptions and competencies that guide good practice. It seems logical that an effective instructor is a competent one when competence is simply defined "as the ability to do a job properly" (Kuruba, 2019, p. 17). In this book, we support the premise that a competent instructor uses skills shown to enhance learning and that the use of instructional competencies can "shift the focus from what instructors should *know* to what instructors should *do*, and potentially even how they should *be*" (Biesta, 2015, p. 3).

Advocating for instructors to be competent on the surface appears reasonable. Yet, how do we define what constitutes a competent instructor? What are the specific instructional skills and abilities needed by today's instructors? Again, we need to think about terms we use and whether there is a difference between *competent* and *competency*. Some dictionaries represent the terms interchangeably, but others, such as Sampson (1998), argue that "there is a real and relevant difference between these two features which, far from being coterminous, describe different aspects, or incremental stages of a person's performance and which therefore have very different functions, competent and competency" (p. 308). According to Sampson, *competence* is assessed with a "yes" or "no" resulting in either someone being competent or not, while competencies reflect variations in levels of performance. Tobias (2006) describes competencies as a set of cognitive, affective, behavioral, and motivational characteristics or dispositions enabling a person to perform well in a situation.

Defining Competency

In describing instructor competence, we recognize that the term competency is defined differently in different contexts; a concise way to define is as "an important skill needed to do a job" (Cambridge Dictionary, n.d.). A broad definition of competencies includes "the collection of success factors necessary for achieving important results in a specific job or work role in a particular organization" (Chouhan & Srivastava, 2014, p. 14). A concise description of competencies, "sets of behaviours that are instrumental in the delivery of desired results or outcomes," was suggested by Bartram et al., (2008, p. 7). Definitional differences are still up for debate, but there is recognition that competency is defined differently in different sectors and contexts. We can identify key characteristics of a competency that include the following:

- consists of one or more skills whose mastery would enable the attainment of the competency;
- links to all three of the domains under which performance can be assessed: knowledge, skills, and attitude; and
- possesses a performance dimension: Competencies are observable and demonstrable; and are observable and measurable (Nessipbayeva, 2012, p. 150).

Paquette (2002) cited a ternary relationship between a skill, knowledge, and public actor or target. It was El Falaki et al. (2010, p. 465) who defined a competency by linking these three aspects:

- Knowledge: Describe the concepts, procedures, principles or specific events which represent domain knowledge.
- Skills: Describe the processes that can be applied to domain knowledge in various fields so that they can be perceived, remembered, assimilated, analyzed and evaluated.
- Public Target: Describe behavioral skills, characteristics, functions and tasks of actors.

In this ongoing quest to appropriately define competency, Asame and Wakrim (2017, p. 228) reviewed competency definitional literature and identified 10 key characteristics that emerged from the literature describing a competency as:

1. a combination of various resources (knowledge, skills, motives, abilities, expertise, traits, values, etc.), which goes beyond a simple possession of these resources;
2. characterized by an integrated series of resources;
3. a process that mobilizes all resources needed to perform a specific task;
4. associated with a certain performance that is ranging from the lowest to the highest proficiency level to classify competency;
5. depends on the specific context in which individuals or employees apply their competencies (in other words, a person can be competent in a context but may not be so in a different context);
6. associated with a situation or family of situations, and it depends on the characteristics of these situations to face the difficult problems in academic or personal reality;

7. depends on the conditions in which it is activated and on the indicators that must determine the construction of the learning activities and of the training programs;
8. related to an actor that may be, for instance, the company, a project team or an individual;
9. finalized and organized in units to attain efficiently a specific objective; and
10. describe the activities specified by a function, a role or a particular task, qualified by the level of excellence of the performance observed and validated by a social sanction.

Based on the above detailed characteristics, Asame and Wakrim (2017) offer this definition: "A set of personal characteristics (skills, knowledge, attitudes, etc.) that a person acquires or needs to acquire, in order to perform an activity inside a certain context with a specific performance level" (p. 228). IBSTPI provides a similar, but less wordy, definition of competency as:

> A set of related knowledge, skills, and attitudes that enable an individual to effectively perform the activities of a given occupation or job function to the standards expected in employment.

The IBSTPI definition is clear, and yet, in the years since it was first written, advances in neuroscience, for example, reveal that the brain is far more malleable than we realized. Due to brain plasticity, connectivity between neurons can change with experience, thus allowing individuals to use strategies that increase our neural growth. Building upon this understanding of our brains, Carol Dweck (2008) coined two terms for the mindsets or beliefs that shape how people approach challenges: A *fixed mindset* views intellect as mostly predetermined and unchangeable, while a *growth mindset* promotes the belief that one improves by putting in extra time and effort. Much of Dweck's work focuses on school-age learners, but it is by no means limited to that audience. Growth mindset approaches are advocated by educators, parents, and professionals, thus prompting an inclusion of mindset in the IBSTPI competency definition: "A set of related knowledge, skills, attitudes and a growth identity that enable an individual to effectively perform the activities of a given occupation or job function to the standards expected in employment."

Identifying Competent Instructors

Advocating for instructors to be competent on the surface appears reasonable. Yet, how do we define what constitutes a competent instructor?

What are the specific instructional skills and abilities needed by today's instructors? Again, we need to think about terms we use and whether there is a difference between competent and competency. When it comes to instructors, we assert that a competent instructor uses knowledge and skills identified to promote learning. Therefore, IBSTPI supports and develops competencies relating to job/role performance that can be measured by standards indicating work performance and not personality traits or beliefs. Support and training can promote development of competence and "at every level, employees learn and develop new competencies starting from unconscious incompetence to conscious competence, and finally expertise in the assigned task" (Salman et al., 2020, p. 723). Our instructional competencies provide a data-driven set of instructional skills and abilities along with a "technology agonistic" perspective in recognition that tools and technologies change. The instructional strategies, however, are relatively stable and adaptable based on new practical and theoretical learnings.

IBSTPI'S INSTRUCTOR COMPETENCIES: THEN AND NOW

In this book, we present an updated and revised set of instructor competencies based on the IBSTPI 2004 set of instructor competencies. IBSTPI first developed and validated a set of instructor competencies in 1988 that was followed by an updated, validated version in 1993. Instruction at that time was predominantly done in classroom settings, but by 2004 the instructional contexts and what we know about how learning works prompted the IBSTPI Board to update the instructor competencies once again. Sets of instructor competencies need to remain current and reflect best practices in our dynamic instructional contexts, and IBSTPI responded to this need by developing and validating the revised set of competencies described in this book.

It isn't just the passage of time since the 2004 version of the competencies that inspired a new set of instructor competencies. We raised many questions that helped guide our competency model revision process. Among our many questions a few repeatedly resurfaced: What advances in society are influencing the instructor standards? What practices and abilities are supported by the current literature findings? Are there changes in instructional fields that may suggest modification to the standards? Do the standards reflect today's differing contexts? Should IBSTPI terminology be better contextualized?

While the initial questions guided our path in exploring the need for a modification to the 2004 instructor competencies, they led to more questions, and deeper exploration of the research led IBSTPI's Board to support a revision of the competences and set them in today's context. Within the following chapters, we will detail the competency model process and our validation process and findings. Our primary purpose of this book is to describe and provide a foundation for the revised IBSTPI instructor competencies. This book offers more than background and supporting literature, for it also suggests how these competencies can be applied to today's instructional contexts. There is a situational and contextual nature to instruction, and that truism is reflected in the competence framework to enable use according to the needs and expertise of instructors.

CONCEPTUALIZING INSTRUCTOR COMPETENCE

Today's instructional landscape is rapidly evolving, and this latest version of the instructor competencies is grounded in research, theory, and evidence-based practices applicable in today's physical and digital learning environments. In the wake of a global pandemic, instructors have been called upon to quickly adapt to new formats and rapidly changing digital tools. What do 21st-century instructors need to be able to know and do to successfully prepare their learners? The IBSTPI competencies, an agreed-upon set of standards for instructional quality intended to be applicable across instructional settings, are categorized into domains. The use of domains facilitates the grouping of competencies by types of activities and an identified theme. The 2004 IBSTPI instructor competencies identified these five domains: Professional Foundations, Planning and Preparation, Instructional Methods and Strategies, Assessment and Evaluation, and Management. Now what we know about instructor competencies has evolved resulting in these four domains: Foundation, Design, Facilitation, and Evaluation. More specifically, when it comes to the Foundation domain, these are the competencies that are somewhat generic in that all instructors need them, but more significantly, they are instructionally foundational. The Design domain clusters the competencies around designing for learning, that is, the work related to preparing for instruction. In essence, it is the *pre-instructional phase* that is followed by the Facilitation domain of instruction. The facilitation of learning is the *instructional phase* where an instructor engages, guides, and assesses learners. The fourth domain, Evaluation, is often the *post-instructional phase* needed to monitor and evaluate instructional effectiveness. The latest IBSTPI domains and competencies reflect the following current key underlying premises impacting teaching and learning. These premises have instructional implications and influence our understanding of what it means to be a competent instructor.

Good Instruction Matters

Research findings indicate that learner achievement is impacted by an instructor's level of competence. Bodies of empirical evidence exist, such as the extensive synthesis of research findings on school-based instructional strategies reported by Hattie and Donoghue. Their research proposed a model of learning comprised of the following three learning inputs and outputs: "student knowledge of the success criteria for the task; three phases of the learning process (surface, deep, and transfer) with surface and deep learning each comprising an acquisition phase and a consolidation phase; and an environment for the learning" (Hattie & Donoghue, 2016, p. 2). Their analysis found a subset of effective strategies that were effectively implemented based on phases of the learning cycle. An effective, competent instructor who has the knowledge, skills, and abilities to incorporate these learning strategies into a variety of instructional contexts and settings positively influences learning. Additionally, attributes that have a meaningful impact on learning are not limited to education; research supports evidence-based training practices that result in effective performance and metrics. Those instructors who are aware of "what works" and in particular "what works best" can effectively instruct in their discipline and contexts and produce results.

Learner Achievement Is Defined and Assessed in Multiple Ways

In the past, assessment was narrowly focused on evaluating learning and comparing performance against a standard or benchmark. Such an approach does not promote the use of data throughout the learning process, and with that limitation in mind, today's instructors are developing alternative methods of assessment that are based on a deeper understanding of how we learn and are used to promote and diagnose learning. Assessment that is integrated into instruction is viewed as integral to the learning process. Simply testing learning is insufficient once we recognize:

> Assessment is the process of gathering and discussing information from multiple and diverse sources in order to develop a deep understanding of what students know, understand and can do with their knowledge as a result of their educational experiences; the process culminates when assessment results are used to improve subsequent learning. (Huba & Freed, 2000, p. 8)

Effective instructors constantly assess student learning using both formative and summative measures. Formative assessments are ongoing and occur during learning to improve learning as well as to help an instructor gauge their own teaching effectiveness. An instructor who checks student progress to provide feedback on what a learner knows or doesn't and provides guidance on how learners can progress, is promoting deeper student understanding. To prove learning occurred, summative assessments are used to measure learning against a standard or a benchmark. While it is possible to use summative assessments in a formative manner, they are mostly limited to guiding revisions and adaptations for the next iteration of the assessment. When assessing learning, competent instructors repeatedly ask, "Are students learning as expected?" and recognize that summative assessments can be value laden. Therefore, what matters is ensuring that the processes of assessment are ethical, transparent, and communicated (Scriven, 1967; Taras, 2009). As a final note, instructors assess learning and additionally are also tasked with evaluating prompting them to identify, improve, and document their instruction. As such, this data-driven approach to instruction is recognized as distinctly different from the assessment of learning.

Focus Instruction on Learning and Not Solely on the Content

By providing instruction based on current science on how our minds learn and think, instructors enable learners to process information and make sense of it. On some levels, this premise sounds rather basic, but it is far more complicated because of the complexity of understanding how learning works. Furthering the complexity of understanding the learning process is that not all possess a common understanding of what constitutes learning. Without a consensus on the definition of learning, there exists an "uncertainty regarding the boundaries of the learning concept and confused assessments about which phenomena genuinely constitute learning" (Barron et al., 2015, p. 2). Despite definitional differences among and within disciplines, a common definition of learning sees it as a processing of information derived from experience to update system properties (Barron et al., 2015). In the field of instruction, a definition of practical utility that we suggest using defines learning "as a process that leads to change, which occurs as a result of experience and increases the potential for improved performance and future learning" (Ambrose et al., 2010, p. 3).

A definitional understanding of learning is the first step for an instructor; they need to learn about theories on learners' construction of beliefs, skills, strategies, and knowledge. Chew and Cerbin (2017) assert that a theory of how we learn is needed to help teachers plan pedagogy more effectively and to gain insights into factors that are relevant to learning. They posit that without an understanding of how learning works, "teachers must make their own assumptions about how students learn. Unfortunately, many teachers base their pedagogy on simplistic ideas, untested intuitions and faulty assumptions" (Chew & Cerbin, 2017, para. 8). A competent instructor keeps abreast of the advances in cognitive science that expand our understanding of individual and specific factors that promote learning. The different learning theories support specific instructional purposes and roles for the instructor. It is up to the instructor to take on the demanding task of translating these theories into practice. By focusing on learning, a competent instructor makes an important assumption: Learners are unique individuals who are capable and willing to learn. Our diverse learners represent a complex landscape of cultural identities. The ability to see learners as individuals with unique needs and characteristics is necessary to provide a positive instructional climate and to instruct inclusively. In a synthesis of current literature on inclusive teaching, Lawrie et al. (2017) writes that conceptualizing, defining, and practicing inclusive teaching and learning will vary depending on the instructor and instructional purposes. Inclusive pedagogy is not prescriptive or a style of teaching, but rather "is a philosophy that forms the basis of pedagogy that recognizes the whole person" (Dewsbury & Brame, 2019, p. 2). An inclusive instructor designs instruction appropriate for different learners, practices reflection, provides classroom interactions open to all, and continually adapts to the changing needs of these learners.

Instructors in Learner-Centered Environments Assume New Roles and Responsibilities

A gradual transformation from an "instructor-centered" approach to a "learner-centered" one is underway in many settings, but it is not universally accepted. According to Kanuka (2010), teacher-centered learning focuses on the experience of teachers or instructors while learner-centered learning is about the experiences of the students. This shift to an instructional model focusing on the learner requires commitment, reframing thinking, and connecting learning research to instructional practice. In response to the learner-centered movement, instructors employ a more active, engaging, collaborative style of instruction. Knowing that instruction is about learning prompts instructors to ask, "How can I improve my students' learning?" instead of the frequently asked, "How can I improve my teaching?" (Weimer, 2002). A learner-centered paradigm promotes more egalitarian learning that enables instructors and learners to be "co-learners." In many instructional settings, however, it is the instructor who is at the center of instructional activity. We are all familiar with a stand-and-delivery mode of instruction (typically called a lecture) that promotes the transmission of information and is recognized as efficient, convenient, and traditional. Lectures, however, are not created or delivered as equals and, in many situations, have been found to be an ineffective way to promote learners' critical thinking, engagement, and self-directed learning. A competent instructor thinks about the learning objectives—that is, what a learner should know and be able to do at the end of instruction—when deciding appropriate pedagogical strategies. A lecture works if an overview of a topic or a model for future activities is needed. Or if your goal is to transmit information and to provide organization and clarity, lectures have been found to be effective (Saroyan, 2000). Advocating for learner-centered instruction does not necessarily suggest one should never lecture. When selecting any instructional method, always keep in mind what it is meant to achieve and the needs of learners. And when electing to lecture, a competent instructor keeps abreast of cognitive science-backed best practices on lecturing and ways to facilitate learner comprehension and retention.

In learner-centered settings, an instructor connects with knowledge and students at the same time (Wohlfarth et al., 2008) to facilitate learning. Instructing is more than knowledge transmission; instead, instructors actively engage learners in the learning process. A caveat does exist: While active learning is any instructional method that engages students, engagement by itself is insufficient. Active learning requires students to perform meaningful learning activities and think about what they are doing (Bonwell & Eison, 1991). Adapting learner-centered approaches extends to all levels of educational programs as well as informal learning and training settings. While many schools and institutions of higher education use learner-centered approaches, it is by no means limited to such settings. For example, in 2011, the U.S. Army's Learning Concept began using learner-centered approaches based on adult education principles and learning theory (Van Der Werff & Bogdan, 2018). Often, instructor development and guidance are needed when transitioning and integrating to learner-centered instruction. Furthermore, successful incorporation of active learning and learner-centered instruction requires buy-in from both instructors and learners (Jackson & Novak, 2018). Engaging learners may also require skills, as suggested by Arghode and Wang (2016), that can be learned and developed, and some are associated with the innate traits of the trainer.

A Competent Instructor Interprets, Selects, and Engages in Evidence-Based Practice

In fields like medicine, social work, and psychology, evidence-based practice (EBP) is deeply rooted; the field of instruction also engages in EBP or, by its other label, evidence-based teaching (EBT). Although Missett and Foster's (2015) definition of EBP focuses on educational settings, it is applicable across instructional contexts: "Broadly speaking, evidence-based practices consist of clearly described curricular interventions, programs, and instructional techniques with methodologically rigorous research bases supporting their effectiveness" (p. 97). Instructors who use effective instructional strategies supported by research and evidence are tasked with identifying and selecting a practice and then implementing it following its intended design. Another essential step in the EBP instructional framework involves evaluating the effectiveness and whether learners are improving. To sum up this breadth of expertise, Scheeler et al. (2016), write: "We view EBP as an empirically validated practice combined with a teacher's professional wisdom to select, use, and analyze such practice" (p. 172). Incorporating EBP into instruction is not trivial, and instructors often need assistance in adapting to these practices. While a body of evidence on best practices for engaging in EBP exists, it is essential to engage in communities of practice and to consistently observe and respond to instructor and learner needs.

Leveraging EBP to enhance instructional effectiveness and facilitate learning transfer has its challenges, however. Despite ongoing efforts to integrate EBP across the instructional landscape, successful implementation of EBP is hindered by a long-standing research-to-practice gap coupled with difficulties in adopting evidence-based-teaching. Pedagogical and social challenges can impede the adoption of EBP in a variety of fields and settings. Among U.S. physics faculty, for example, a national survey found that while 87% reported knowledge of evidence-based strategies, only 50% reported adopting these practices (Henderson & Dancy, 2009). There are numerous reasons this situation exists (i.e., lack of training, misunderstanding of EBT), and across instructional contexts many issues remain in the successful process and implementation of EBT. Translating research to practice is challenging and requires an openness to instructional experimentation. An ability to accept diverse ways of knowing and willingness to be a reflective practitioner are also essential. By engaging in critical and reflective thinking, instructors can thoughtfully adjust to the learning curve that comes with EBT.

These premises by no means represent the scope of current understandings on teaching and learning. They do, however, speak to fundamental factors that are evident not only in the literature, but in practice. And they strongly influence and underpin this latest revision of IBSTPI's instructor competency model, which contains domains, competencies, and performance statements. The domains, clusters of related competencies, are categorized by an area of activity along with a theme. These domains, competencies, and accompanying performance statements all represent the standards detailed within this book.

INSTRUCTIONAL TECHNOLOGIES AND LEARNING MODALITIES

We live in a digital age with an abundant access to information that drives change and innovation. For many sectors of our economy, rapid change is the norm. Instructional enterprises, however, tend to be less nimble in this changing learning landscape. Although change and innovation do impact how we instruct and learn in our global learning society, those with capital and resources have the most access to advanced technologies. While the future is always uncertain, it is expected to experience a transformational change in how society teaches, learns, and prepares the workforce (Greenhow et al., 2009). Substantive change, across the globe, faces a myriad of challenges; a primary concern is the inadequacies of a task-centric approach to instruction (Boston & Smith, 2011). To meet these challenges, a move from a dated instructional focus on knowledge acquisition and task readiness is needed. It is time to adapt because "teachers and students need access to current, readily accessible information and competencies that prepare them for the knowledge age. While in our workforce, workers need to learn and adapt their knowledge and skills as tools and job expectations evolve" (Tucker et al., 2020, p. 2). A desire and an openness to change not only what is taught, but why and how it is taught, are a necessary step to enable technology to change what instructors and learners do.

New tools and technologies are agents of change in many aspects of modern life; many predict that our relationships with technology will become even more deeply integrated into how we live, learn, work, and play. Technology is in our lives, and some contend that we live in two worlds: analog and digital. While there are many benefits to a technology-infused lifestyle, there are concerns that a "tele-everything" world contributes to economic inequality, overly powerful big technology firms, and increases in the spread of misinformation (Anderson et al., 2021). Across the globe, despite the uneven distribution across ethnic, socioeconomic, and geographic lines of digital tools and instructional technologies, it is increasingly apparent that instructing and learning in today's world demands competency with digital tools and technologies. Advocacy for the use of these technologies and tools needs to be strongly rooted in decision-making based on ethics and equity of access. Selection and use of the unprecedented range of digital tools and technologies are not trivial tasks; instructors and those who support instruction must seek answers as to how technologies bring pedagogical, economic, and value-added benefits. Instructors also need to be comfortable experimenting and using a variety of technologies.

How can we use instructional technologies to create effective learning experiences? Such an encompassing question can't lead to a simplistic answer or one this book intends to address in detail. The effective use of technologies resulting in increased learning is dependent on many variables and raises issues such as these basic questions: "Will the technology/tool support attainment of the learning objectives?"; "Can the instructional affordances and features of the technology support the pedagogical approaches?"; and "What is expected of an instructor in terms of roles and skills?" First and foremost, however, it needs to be noted that problems ensue when pedagogical and instructional design decisions are centered on a particular technology. Instructors should select the technology based upon well-defined learning objectives and be able to make an informed choice by staying abreast of emerging new technology-assisted ways of learning trends and practices.

Innovative technologies can provide novel and powerful learning experiences with opportunities for collaborative, interactive, and adaptive learning. Bear in mind that today's dynamic technologies are often in a stage of flux in a highly competitive marketplace, and ongoing scrutiny is needed to even just stay current. Furthermore, instructional technologies decision-making involves stakeholder input, which may or may not include instructors' voices. These decision-making processes are context specific, and if we look to decision-makers in American K–12 organizations, as an example, we find a tendency to get three perspectives: local knowledge, data, and scientifically based research (Hollands & Escueta, 2020). In these organizations, the findings are contextualized with "local data analyses, organizational history, and practice experience" (Tseng & Nutley, 2014, p. 170), which facilitates an instructor playing a role and contributing to technology decision-making. How involved an instructor is in technology decision-making is context specific, but it is essential that all instructors know how to selectively use technology in meaningful ways to support learning and the learner's needs. Simply put, competent instructors prioritize the learners while capitalizing on the technology.

INSTRUCTIONAL ROLES AND SETTINGS

Today's instructional policies, practice, and emerging technologies influence changes in instructor roles, tools, and settings. The newly revised instructor competency standards within this book are adaptations of the ones identified in the 2004 version of the instructor competencies. At that time, instructional learning environments were identified as face-to-face, blended, and online. For the most part, that configuration continues today, but with nuanced differences. A face-to-face distinction is no longer made and instead has morphed into foundational competencies germane to all who instruct. That is, the Foundation domain assumes expected competence in the performance of instructor duties regardless of the specific domains of instructor responsibilities. It does not repeat competencies specific to the other domains because it assumes demonstrated competent practice across all domains. Much of today's instruction occurs in either blended or online environments. Blended or hybrid settings combine traditional, place-based instruction with digital and online opportunities for learning. Online settings are those that deliver fully virtual instruction via the internet using a variety of technologies and tools. Both blended and online offer synchronous and asynchronous learning opportunities. In these settings, an instructor often interacts and collaborates with others, including, for example, instructional designers, media specialists, assessment experts, other instructors, and so on.

Blended Settings

Blended learning means different things to different people. This lack of consensus on its definition has persisted for many years. According to Friesen (2012), it is difficult to pinpoint when the term *blended learning* was coined. In 1999, however, the EPIC Learning Center offered an ambiguous definition resulting in conceptualizing blended learning as "almost any combination of technologies, pedagogies and even job tasks. It includes some of the oldest mechanical media (e.g., film) and theories of learning (e.g., behaviorism), as well as the newest" (Friesen, 2012, p. 2). In the decade or so since Friesen proposed that definition, blended learning is now prevalent in more and more instructional contexts. Yet, despite a recognition that "the complexities of blending learning go far beyond deciding between face-to-face and technology-mediated contact" (Cronje, 2020, p. 115), we continue to need a better definition of blended learning. When defining blended learning, the delivery medium need not be specified, for "it is the context, rather than the meaning, that makes a difference. A definition of blended learning should focus on learning" (Cronje, 2020, p. 117). Cronje (2020) additionally offers this succinct definition: "The appropriate use of a mix of theories, methods and technologies to optimise learning in a given context" (p. 120). This definition resonates with how blended learning is presented in this book, and it aligns with IBSTPI's instructor competencies.

Many instructors through the years have mixed delivery and interaction modes, but today's competent instructors are designing and delivering blended learning based on best instructional practices and a greater understanding of how learning works. The adoption of technology into a traditional course, such as the use of social media tools, is on the low end of the blended learning continuum. More complex, fully blended learning places new demands on instructors and requires more intentionally designed instruction than in a face-to-face course environment.

Online Settings

Online learning, like blended learning, does not have a single definition or label. Some prominent examples include calling it a form of distance learning, e-learning, or web-based learning. Although there are numerous definitions and conceptualizations of online learning, technology is prominent in all by "describing how technology delivers content, enhances the existing learning environment, and enhances the interactions among the students or teachers" (Singh & Thurman, 2019, p. 293). In fully online instructional settings, instructors and learners connect via technology and are not physically in the same environment. In our Information Age with ongoing technology developments, the delivery and strategies of online learning are rapidly evolving. The internet allowed us to connect virtually; thus, online learning was not only possible, but in many instances, preferable. The idea that learning could occur anywhere and anytime has appeal, for it opens learning pathways for diverse and dispersed learners. We've also witnessed the necessity of separating instructors and learners during the COVID-19 pandemic, when many were thrust into teaching and learning via technology. Confusion about what constitutes online learning existed before the spring of 2020, but the term *online learning* became an umbrella term for many types of remote instruction.

In a systematic literature review of the definitions of online learning, Singh and Thurman (2019) identified these common elements:

- Technology is a crucial part of the definition.
- A lack of clearly defined terms exists.
- The confusion exists due to many overlapping and/or distinct concepts presented in definitions as synonyms.
- Some definitions include time with mentions of synchronous and asynchronous elements.
- Some include interactivity as an important aspect.
- Physical distance is not always included as an element, but it is mentioned consistently.
- Educational context, such as formal or higher education settings, may be mentioned.

Just as Cronje found when reviewing blended learning definitions, Singh and Thurman found that online learning definitions do not describe learning. They, however, assert that learning is not integral to a conceptual understanding of online learning and instead advocate for options in defining online learning. While definitions of online learning continue to evolve, those in the field of online teaching and learning are intent on making a distinction between instruction conducted over the internet and instruction designed for online learning in a student-centric learning environment. With the complexities of online teaching and learning in mind, we find the following definition aligns with our vision of online learning: "Online learning uses the internet as a delivery modality to offer thoughtfully designed, quality, student-focused learning experiences, built on proven best practices that create effective interactions between learners, peers, instructors, and content" (Mathes, 2020, para. 5).

An online instructor's roles and responsibilities are not the same as those teaching in traditional settings. In some settings, such as in traditional classrooms, instructors may know their content but do not know best instructional practices. All instructors have been students and therefore some go on the assumption that you can teach as you were taught. While this is a faulty assumption in traditional instructional settings, it rarely rings true for online learning. For starters, many instructors have never been online learners, and without any familiarity with online learning, instructors need assistance in adapting pedagogically, socially, and technologically. Next, online learning environments don't replicate traditional instructional offerings and instead require both instructor and learners to adjust to new roles and expectations. Additionally, instructional design and planning are paramount to quality instruction, but when it comes to online instruction, it is typically developed far in advance of delivery and often involves a team of instructional developers. Instructors are expected to interact with a range of technology and pedagogy specialists and to iteratively design instruction before it is "tested live." Typically, online instructors are tasked with assuming five different roles: facilitator, course designer, content manager, subject matter expert, and mentor (Martin et al., 2019). During online instruction, instructors are to be present and to primarily facilitate, guide and direct learners.

CONCLUSION

In this introductory chapter, you are prompted to think about instructor competencies and whether your understanding aligns with current findings and terminology. By coming to a shared understanding of what is meant by basic terms such as instructor, learner, or competency, we can develop a shared understanding of the relevancy of instructor competency efforts. We use the term instructor because it is synonymous with numerous types of educators including, for example, trainers, mentors, or tutors. If you instruct, the competencies described in this book are appropriate for you. The competencies can be applied to instructors in settings with or without technology and are appropriate when instructing diverse learners of all levels.

REFERENCES

Ambrose, S., Bridges, M., DiPietro, M., Lovett, M., & Norman, M. (2010). *How learning works: Seven research-based principles for smart teaching*. Jossey-Bass.

Anderson, J., Raine, L., & Vogels, E. (2021, February 18). *Experts say the "new normal" in 2025 will be far more tech-driven, presenting more big challenges*. Pew Research Center. https://www.pewresearch.org/internet/2021/02/18/experts-say-the-new-normal-in-2025-will-be-far-more-tech-driven-presenting-more-big-challenges/

Arghode, V., & Wang, J. (2016). Exploring trainers' engaging instructional practices: A collective case study. *European Journal of Training and Development, 40*(2), 111–127. https://doi.org/10.1108/EJTD-04-2015-0033

Asame, M., & Wakrim, M. (2017). Towards a competency model: A review of the literature and the competency standards. *Education and Information Technologies, 23*, 225–236. https://doi.org/10.1007/s10639-017-9596-z

Barron, A., Hebets, E., Cleland, T., Fitzpatrick, C., Hauber, M., & Stevens, J. (2015). Embracing multiple definitions of learning. *Trends in Neurosciences, 38*(7), 405–407. https://doi.org/10.1016/j.tins.2015.04.008

Bartram, D., Robertson, I. T., & Callinan, M. (2008). Introduction: A framework for examining organizational effectiveness. In I. T. Robertson, M. Callinan, & D. Bartram (Eds.), *Organizational effectiveness: The role of psychology* (pp. 1–10). Wiley. http://doi.org/10.1002/9780470696736.ch

Biesta, G. J. J. (2015). How does a competent teacher become a good teacher? On judgement, wisdom and virtuosity in teaching and teacher education. In R. Heilbronn & L. Foreman-Peck (Eds.), *Philosophical perspectives on the future of teacher education* (pp. 3–22). Wiley Blackwell.

Bonwell, C., & Eison, J. (1991). *Active learning: Creating excitement in the classroom. 1991 ASHE-ERIC Higher Education Reports*. School of Education and Human Development, George Washington University. https://eric.ed.gov/?id=ED336049

Boston, M. D., & Smith, M. S. (2011). A "task-centric approach" to professional development: Enhancing and sustaining mathematics teachers' ability to implement cognitively challenging mathematical tasks. *ZDM, 43*, 965–977.

Cambridge Dictionary. (n.d.). Competency. In *Cambridge dictionary*. Retrieved July 14, 2022 from https://dictionary.cambridge.org/us/dictionary/english/competency

Chew, S. L., & Cerbin, W. J. (2017, December 5). *Teaching and learning: Lost in a buzzword wasteland*. Inside Higher Ed. https://www.insidehighered.com/views/2017/12/05/need-theory-learning-opinion

Chouhan, V., & Srivastava, S. (2014). Understanding competencies and competency modeling—A literature survey. *ISOR Journal of Business and Management, 16*(1), 14–22. https://doi.org/10.9790/487X-16111422

Cronje, J. (2020). Towards a new definition of blended learning. *The Electronic Journal of e-Learning, 18*(2), 114–121.
Dewsbury, B., & Brame, C. J. (2019). Inclusive teaching. *CBE Life Sciences Education, 18*(2). https://doi.org/10.1187/cbe.19-01-0021
Dweck, C. S. (2008). *Mindset: The new psychology of success.* Ballantine Books.
El Falaki, B., Khalidi, M., & Bennani, S., (2010). A formative assessment model within the competency-based-approach for an individualized e-learning path. *World Academy of Science, Engineering and Technology, International Journal of Social, Behavioral, Educational, Economic, Business and Industrial Engineering, 4*(4), 464–468. https://www.researchgate.net/publication/286039295
Friesen, N. (2012, August). *Report: Defining blended learning.* https://www.normfriesen.info/papers/Defining_Blended_Learning_NF.pdf
Greenhow, C., Robelia, B., & Hughes, J. E. (2009). Learning, teaching, and scholarship in a digital age: Web 2.0 and classroom research: What path should we take now? *Educational Researcher, 38*(4), 246–259. https://doi.org/10.3102/0013189X09336671
Hattie, J., & Donoghue, G. (2016). Learning strategies: A synthesis and conceptual model. *NPJ Science of Learning, 1,* 16013. https://doi.org/10.1038/npjscilearn.2016.13
Henderson, C., & Dancy, M. (2009). Impact of physics education research on the teaching of introductory quantitative physics in the United States. *Physical Review Physics Education Research, 5*(2). https://journals.aps.org/prper/abstract/10.1103/PhysRevSTPER.5.020107
Hollands, F., & Escueta, M. (2020). How research informs educational technology decision-making in higher education: The role of external research versus internal research. *Educational Technology Research and Development, 68,* 163–180. https://doi.org/10.1007/s11423-019-09678-z
Huba, M., & Freed, J. (2000). *Learner-centered assessment on college campuses: Shifting the focus from teaching to learning.* Allyn & Bacon.
Jackson, K., & Novak, D. (2018, June 7). *3 strategies for overcoming faculty resistance to active learning techniques.* Educause Review. https://er.educause.edu/blogs/2018/6/3-strategies-for-overcoming-faculty-resistance-to-active-learning-techniques
Kanuka, H. (2010). Characteristics of effective and sustainable teaching development programmes for quality teaching in higher education. *Higher Education Management and Policy, 22*(2), 1–14. https://doi.org/10.1787/hemp-22-5kmbq08ncr25
Kuruba, M. (2019). *Role competency matrix: A step-by-step guide to an objective competency management system.* Springer.
Lawrie, G., Marquis, E., Fuller, E., Newman, T., Qiu, M., Nomikoudis, M., Roelofs, F., & van Dam, L. (2017). Moving towards inclusive learning and teaching: A synthesis of recent literature. *Teaching & Learning Inquiry, 5*(1) 9–21. http://doi.org/10.20343/teachlearninqu.5.1.3
Ludwikowska, K. (2018). Evidence based training approach in organizational practice. *Modern Management Review, 25*(4), 117–131. http://doi.org/10.7862/rz.2018.mmr.48

Marsh, H., Morin, A., Ginns, P., Nagengast, B., & Martin, A. (2011). Use of student ratings to benchmark universities: Multilevel modeling of responses to the Australian course experience questionnaire (CEQ). *Journal of Educational Psychology, 103*(3), 733–748. https://doi.org/10.1037/a0024221

Martin, F., Budhrani, K., Kumar, S., & Ritzhaupt, A. (2019). Award-winning faculty online teaching practices: Roles and competencies. *Online Learning, 23*(1), 184–205. http://doi.org/10.24059/olj.v23i1.1329

Mathes, J. (2020, April 13). *A defining moment for online learning.* The OLC Blog. https://onlinelearningconsortium.org/a-defining-moment-for-online-learning/?gclid=CjwKCAjwyIKJBhBPEiwAu7zllzTCxVsAuieeCrh2JP0cu4At9C_aQnJk1uUQLTbusrDC-O6jhqZRfRoC8ZsQAvD_BwE

Missett, T., & Foster, L. (2015). Searching for evidence-based practice: A survey of empirical studies on curricular interventions measuring and reporting fidelity of implementation published during 2004–2013. *Journal of Advanced Academics, 26,* 96–111. https://doi.org/10.1177/1932202X15577206

Nessipbayeva, O. (2012). The competencies of the modern teacher. In N. Popov, C. Wolhuter, B. Leutwyler, G. Hilton, J. Ogunleye, & P. A. Almedia (Eds.), *International perspectives on education: BCES conference books, 10,* 148–154. Bulgarian Comparative Education Society. https://eric.ed.gov/?id=ED567040

Paquette, G. (2002). *Modeling knowledge and skills to design and learn* (1st ed.). Press of the University of Quebec. https://doi.org/10.2307/j.ctv18ph0w2

Salman, M., Ganie, S. A., & Saleen, I. (2020). The concept of competence: A thematic review and discussion. *European Journal of Training and Development, 44*(6–7), 717–742. https://doi.org/10.1108/EJTD-10-2019-0171

Sampson, F. (1998). Competence or competency: What's in a word? *The Police Journal, 71*(4), 307–309. https://doi.org/10.1177/0032258X9807100404

Saroyan, A. (2000). Addressing the needs of large groups. The lecturer. In J. Bess (Ed.), *Teaching alone/teaching together: Transforming the structure of teams for teaching.* Jossey-Bass.

Scheeler, M., Budin, S., & Markelz, A. (2016). The role of teacher preparation in promoting evidence-based practice in schools. *Learning Disabilities: A Contemporary Journal, 14*(2), 171–187. https://files.eric.ed.gov/fulltext/EJ1118433.pdf

Scriven, M. (1967). The methodology of evaluation. In R. Tyler, R. Gagné, & M. Scriven (Eds.), *Perspectives of curriculum evaluation* (pp. 39–83). Rand McNally.

Seidel, T., & Shavelson, R. (2007). Teaching effectiveness research in the past decade: The role of theory and research design in disentangling research results. *Review of Educational Research, 77*(4), 454–499. https://doi.org/10.3102/0034654307310317

Singh, V., & Thurman, A. (2019). How many ways can we define online learning? A systematic literature review of definitions of online learning (1988–2018). *American Journal of Distance Education, 33*(4), 289–306. https://doi.org/10.1080/08923647.2019.1663082

Taras, M. (2009). Summative and formative assessment: Perceptions and realities. *Active Learning in Higher Education, 9*(2), 172–192. https://doi.org/10.1177/1469787408091655

The Glossary of Education Reform. (2014, April 21). *Learner*. https://www.edglossary.org/learner/

Tobias, L. (2006). *Organizational competence management—A competence performance approach.* Shaker.

Tseng, V., & Nutley, S. (2014). Building the infrastructure to improve the use and usefulness of research in education. In K. S. Finnigan & A. J. Daly (Eds.), *Using research evidence in education: From the schoolhouse door to Capitol Hill* (pp. 163–175). Springer.

Tucker, C., & Jackson, K. S., & Park, J. J. (2020, June). *Exploring the future of engineering education: Perspectives from a workshop on artificial intelligence and the future of STEM and societies* [Paper presentation]. ASEE Virtual Annual Conference. https://par.nsf.gov/servlets/purl/10211081

Van Der Werff, J., & Bogdan, E. (2018, April). Fostering instructor competencies through Army University's faculty development program. *Journal of Military Learning*, 44–52. https://www.armyupress.army.mil/Journals/Journal-of-Military-Learning/Journal-of-Military-Learning-Archives/April-2018-Edition/Fostering-Instructor-Competencies-through-Army-Universitys-Faculty-Development-Program/

Weimer, M. (2002). *Learner-centered teaching: Five key changes to practice.* Jossey-Bass.

Wohlfarth, D., Sheras, D., Bennett, J., Simon, B., Pimentel, J., & Gabel, L. (2008). Student perceptions of learner-centered teaching. *InSight: A Journal of Scholarly Teaching, 3*, 67–74. http://doi.org/10.46504/03200808wo

CHAPTER 2

INSTRUCTOR COMPETENCIES DEVELOPMENT MODEL

OVERVIEW

The first chapter in this book describes the concept of competence and its application in the field by those who instruct. Although instructors work in many settings and contexts, that does not mean there isn't overlap in the knowledge, skills, and attitudes (KSAs) needed to be a competent instructor. While clarification of the theoretical and conceptual understanding of how to identify a competent instructor remains ongoing, competency models can provide frameworks for identifying and describing the KSAs for instructors. This chapter begins with an introduction to competency model development. The focus of this chapter, however, is on the IBSTPI competency model: its development process and how it was applied to identify and validate the instructor competencies.

Orienting Questions

- What are competency models?
- What is the IBSTPI competency development model?
- How was the IBSTPI competency development model applied to instructor competencies?

COMPETENCY MODEL DEVELOPMENT

We would need to go back in time at least 50 years ago if we wanted to find a time that predates the use of competencies and competency models. In the ensuing years, competencies have become expected practice in many fields, as indicated by the proliferation of definitions, tools, models, and applications (Vazirani, 2010). Despite sector- and context-specific perspectives resulting in differing views on the concept of competency, there are some convergent perspectives (Salman et al., 2020). A review of how researchers and practitioners operationalize the term *competency* by Arifin and colleagues (2017, p. 1204) identified these three main definitional positions:

- to measure individual performance,
- the important criteria or elements of the outcome of the person's performance, and
- the characteristics of a person to perform in a job or profession.

In addition to the definitional perspectives, another consideration is the conceptual complexity of competence. To be professionally competent is multifaceted, given that it involves "the ability to solve ambiguous problems, tolerate uncertainty, and make decisions with limited information" (Epstein & Hundert, 2002, p. 227). Basically, competencies are indicators of a capability or an ability; however, a demonstration of a behavior might be based on multiple reasons and due to various intended results (Boyatzis, 2009). Furthermore, competencies are not fixed resources, but instead are ones that can be learned in order to cultivate complex abilities that result in real-life situational behaviors. A distinct advantage of a competency or behavioral approach is that an individual has agency and the ability to develop new competencies or to gain a higher level of competency. In advocating for competencies with proficiency levels, Fink (2017) writes that "competencies also serve as career development tools, illuminating areas for growth, learning objectives for training, and priorities for high-potential programs and talent pipelines" (p. 22).

A challenge with the use of competencies is the difficulty of determining whether workers possess the competencies critical for success. This complex challenge prompted the realization that a scientific, systematic approach to the study of competencies is needed. In an effort to develop new approaches to predict individuals' performance, psychologist David McClelland (1973) and a research team developed the first competency model designed for use in the selection of junior U.S. Foreign Service officers. A competency model "can be considered as a generic structure which is applicable beyond the built environment professions," and should contain these elements: a name for the competence; a description of the competence;

a proficiency level of the context; and context (Sampson & Frytros, 2008, p. 166). Competency models are proliferating into multiple models to represent the collection of competencies illustrating the knowledge, skills, abilities, and other characteristics (KSAOs) germane to effective performance in a profession or work setting. These models offer guidance for what success looks like by describing effective skills and capabilities needed for a particular job or role, in a particular organization or profession.

In the years preceding their initial usage, competency models have generated a body of evidence-based knowledge from studies of numerous job fields, including engineering, management, scientific research, and technical jobs (Megahed, 2018). Current understanding based on the competency modeling literature is still emerging, however; it is evident that there is a need to address gaps in the research knowledge and applicability of the models (Megahed, 2018).

Job competencies differ from job analysis of tasks and skills and instead include "the related knowledge, skills, abilities, and attributes that form a person's job" (Sanghi, 2016, p. 24). Job analysis is no longer as prevalent in the workplace, and Sanghi (2016) credits the widespread adoption of competency modeling to these primary uses: provides more interesting insights about personal characteristics and outstanding performance; offers a unifying conceptual framework for HR functions; and can facilitate organizational change.

Job analysis and competency modeling also differ in methodological approaches, with earlier findings indicating that typical competency modeling was less rigorous than job analysis (Shippmann et al., 2000). Competency modeling, however, is evolving and can be rigorously conducted. Multiple approaches to competency modeling exist, and we need to recognize that "much like a job analysis procedure, if proper processes are put into place and best practices followed, a competency model can have just as much rigor and documentation as a job analysis" (Thompson et al., 2017, p. 6).

Instructor Competency Models

Initially, the study of competencies focused on individual competencies; however, in the 1990s, competency models emerged. Basically, a competency model or framework groups together key competencies required for a job and defines successful job performance. Such comprehensive lists of competencies and performance behaviors are pivotal to a profession and can serve as markers for professional achievement (Drisko, 2014). Additionally, a range of competencies is identified with assessment measures that "reflect a developmental progression in competence, not simply to show its presence or absence" (Drisko, 2014, p. 418). Instructors' professional knowledge and skills encompass "cognitive aspects (e.g., professional knowledge), beliefs related to learning, and motivational and self-regulatory variables" (Kunter et al., 2013, p. 805) and, notably, are recognized as knowledge and skills that can be taught versus innate characteristics.

As professionals, instructors and trainers work in a wide range of settings that require the knowledge of teaching. This knowledge was not clearly understood, however. That limitation was addressed in 1986, when Shulman (1986) urged for the professionalization of teaching by going beyond pedagogical knowledge (PK) and introducing pedagogical content knowledge (PCK), the blending of pedagogy and subject content matter. Succinctly put, PCK is the "what" and "how" of teaching. Competent instructors possess theoretical and practical knowledge, but that alone is not sufficient in today's instructional settings infused with technology: Instructors need additional knowledge and skills. Instructing requires the ability to act appropriately in a dynamic, complex situation supported by the abilities to employ technology knowledge (TK), which includes knowledge of basic technologies (e.g., chalkboards), more advanced technologies (e.g., the Internet), and various modalities for representing information (Polly et al., 2010). While Shulman connected knowledge of pedagogy to a specific content, additional models by Mishra and Koehler (2007) added to our understanding by identifying technological pedagogical knowledge (TPACK) as an instructor's ability to recognize the affordance and constraints of technologies used to deliver instruction and the model. An additional model, pedagogical technology integration content knowledge (PTICK), developed by Brantley-Dias et al. (2007) includes procedural, conceptual, and pedagogical knowledge, but also includes reflective and community knowledge relating to technology integration. Instructors who use technology in instruction can use these frameworks to integrate what is being taught, how it is being taught, and the relationships between technological tools and pedagogical practices. Instructors need a deep knowledge base, and with the rapidly changing technology-driven, external environment that seeps into our lives and workplaces, it is clear there is a need to identify and adapt instructor competencies to meet these demands. A solution to the development of appropriate and relevant competencies is through the use of systematic and valid competency models.

Competency models are useful in various sectors where instruction and training occur in higher education, industry, government, K–12 settings, and nonprofit organizations. Instructors identify and develop competencies for learners, but there are also instructor competencies which are developed through training/education, professional practice, and lifelong learning. A review of competency models in different fields by Staskevica (2019) identified these three advantages to competency models in academia: development and skills of abilities of students; improvement and quality of effectiveness of teaching; and process optimization of standards. Beyond academia, various instructor competency models are available, including, for example, the competencies for performance and learning professionals developed by the Institute for Performance and Learning (I4PL) and the Association for Talent Development's model (ATD) consisting of generic competencies and job-specific ones. In this book, we are presenting the IBSTPI's instructor competencies that use a generic competency development model to provide a base set of standards for instructional quality across instructional settings. By leveraging levels of analysis when defining the competencies, the IBSTPI model "puts into perspective the link between the competencies, the job role, and how each competency is demonstrated" (Koszalka et al., 2013, p. 10).

THE IBSTPI COMPETENCY DEVELOPMENT MODEL

In the years since the IBSTPI board was incorporated in 1984, this organization has steadily followed a rigorous competency development process. Using a competency model, IBSTPI has developed numerous competencies standards including evaluator competencies (Russ-Eft et al., 2014), instructional design competencies (Koszalka et al., 2013), instructor competencies (Klein et al., 2004), online learner competencies (Beaudoin et al., 2013), and training manager competencies (Foxon et al., 2003). IBSTPI's competency model however is dynamic and can be adapted to leverage emerging pedagogical evidence-based findings and to reflect today's dynamic instructional contexts. Before detailing how IBSTPI's competency model was revised and how it framed the development of the 2021 instructor competencies, some background on the IBSTPI competency development model is needed.

Job Role

In brief, applying the competency model begins with defining the job role. A job role is context-dependent, but these roles have overlapping job responsibilities, standards of performance, and ethics and values along with a future vision. In 2013, IBSTPI slightly modified its 2004 generic competency model to provide a framework for instructional designers that includes performance indicators as essential, advanced, or managerial. The IBSTPI competency development model, shown in Figure 2.1, does not include the managerial performance indicator because instructor job roles are not managerial in nature and instead reveals how the job role, competencies, and demonstration of competencies are linked. Underlying this model is the premise that refinement, as an iterative process, will occur.

28 • Instructor Competencies

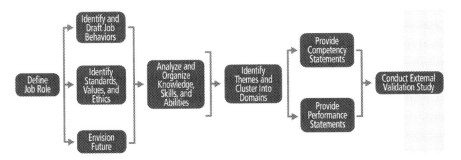

Figure 2.1 The IBSTPI competency development model.

The IBSTPI generic competency model illustrated above starts with defining a job role to identify the function or the purpose of a job. This definition is dependent upon the job setting, and it is likely that one size does not fit all when it comes to job roles. Thus, IBSTPI uses generalized views of job roles in its model, given that most professionals work in a variety of organized settings where one may or may not need each of the identified competencies. When it comes to instructors, for example, it isn't reasonable to narrowly define job roles, so IBSTPI employs the use of a broad conception of being an instructor.

Job Behaviors

The next process in the model questions what is required to successfully perform in a job role. The model's approach addresses job behaviors by identifying and drafting competencies that are statements of performance and which exclude personality traits or beliefs. A review of existing standards and current practice is undertaken, and due to IBSTPI's expertise in this field, this process often begins with reviewing an existing set of IBSTPI standards. Are modifications needed? IBSTPI does not have a timeline cycle for revising its standards but instead conducts periodic preliminary probes of current literature, insights from experts in the field, and emerging workplace practices and tools to ascertain whether a revision of existing competencies is merited. It is essential to explore whether there have been changes to job roles, theories, technologies, and practices in the field that impact instructor competencies. The competencies are designed to adapt to educational trends and technologies, given that competent professionals keep current on new trends and can therefore adapt to changing tools and technologies.

Accepted Standards, Values, and Ethics

While identifying job behaviors is essential in this model, job behaviors are insufficient by themselves: The necessary professional values and ethics must be identified, as well as the standards of performance. Is the competency essential for all jobs, or is it one that is found in a more advanced role? One size does not fit all when it comes to job roles; what an instructor actually does in contemporary practice is context-specific and most likely calls for performing in new and complex ways.

Vision of the Future

There are many levels of complexity impacting instructor's KSAs due to emerging trends in evidence-based practices and technological tools thus requiring the model to include a predictive look into the future to give shape and direction to what will be needed to be effective in a job role. This stage of analysis is critical, for it calls for judgments as to what the role is or should be. As described in *Instructional Designer Competencies*, "It is the tension between what is and what should be and an analysis of trends and expectations of future visions of how the instructional designer role will develop over the next 5 to 10 years that influence the definition of the competencies" (Koszalka et al., 2013, p. 11).

Validated Knowledge, Skills, and Attitudes

The analysis and empirical process begins with job role definition and then specifies current practice and existing standards facilitating competency development. It is within the structure of the IBSTPI competency model that a job role is analyzed, studied, and organized into domains, competencies, and performance statements. A review of literature and current practice is conducted to ensure best practices, and empirical evidence grounds the knowledge base for updating the competencies. This examination process entails more than reviewing research findings, for it also involves reviewing documents or materials in use in various contexts such as corporate, academic, or governmental environments.

Domains of Performance

Domains are clusters of related competencies with an identified theme. The 2022 IBSTPI instructor competencies are grouped into these domains that reveal the relationship between competencies: foundation, design, facilitation, and evaluation. Competencies that instructionally underpin the Foundation domain. The Design domain's competencies are those needed in the planning and preparing for instruction and learning, while the Facilitation domain clusters competencies in which an instructor engages, guides, and assesses learners. The Evaluation domain provides competencies to monitor and evaluate instructional effectiveness.

Competencies and Performance Statements

At the core of the competency model are competencies statements providing short, general descriptions of a complex effort. An explanation of how the competency is demonstrated is provided through a performance statement. It is during a systematic and iterative process that the KSAs are reviewed, deliberated, and rewritten. These derived competencies and statements reflect the understandings and perspectives of the board and outside experts and are intended to consistently and clearly communicate to a broad audience. Using this revised list, a validation study is conducted by an external audience, who rate the criticality of each competency and performance statement.

APPLYING THE MODEL TO INSTRUCTOR COMPETENCIES

Reviewing the 2004 Competencies

A process to review the 2004 version of the IBSTPI instructor competencies was initiated. An IBSTPI team of four people agreed to review the competencies, and if deemed appropriate, revise the set. Going into this review, preliminary thinking was that the revision would not need to be substantial, but that a thorough review process must first be completed. The instructor competencies' review process used the following steps: extensive discussions of the current version of the competencies; identifying and reviewing current literature; scrutinizing versions of published instructor competencies (or similar works) from across the globe; informally discussing the changing role of the instructors with experts on the board and from outside the board; and drafting recommendations on how to proceed. Specifically, the first phase of the process for the review of the 2004 standards went as follows:

- thorough examination of the (2004) instructor competencies;
- literature review of current instructional strategies and tools/technologies, assessment and evaluation practices, and instructional contexts/environments;

- analysis of competencies/performance statements' similarities and differences in contrasting learning settings;
- review of the brief descriptions of the performance statements for each competency and learning setting; and
- discussions to resolve which competencies were outdated, unclear, no longer needed, or missing.

The initial review team of four IBSTPI current/former directors determined that a major effort was needed to update the terminology of the standards, revise the competencies and performance statements to address changes in the roles of instructors, and modify the format in which the standards would be presented. These significant modifications would bring the standards up to date and present them in a way that better fit instructors' needs in today's world. The review team surmised that the existing format was not flexible enough to support instructors in general or to address specific instructor roles in either enhancing instruction with technology or in online settings.

Revising the Competencies Framework

The team began creating a new framework that would better capture instructor foundational skills applicable in most settings and the context-specific skills needed in blended and online environments. A tree structure was used to model the framework for updating the instructor competencies. This visual (Figure 2.2) guided discussion, and we reviewed and revised the organization of the standards into domains, competencies, performance statements, and descriptors. The tree structure not only illustrates how the instructor competencies are organized and connected but can also symbolize professional growth. The tree's *roots* are the ethical foundations that all instructors need as a basis for practice. *Limbs,* larger branches on a tree, represent the domains, but because domains are grouped into clusters of related competencies, the tree model has *offshoots.* The 2004 competencies are the basis of the updated set of competencies; however, the competencies are devised specifically to address each one of the three following learning settings: general learning (generic); technology-enhanced learning settings; and online learning settings. The three initial settings were refined, however, and are described in the following paragraph on drafting the updated competencies. Stemming from the offshoot are the *twigs* with performance statements that express the way each specific competency can be demonstrated. The *foliage* represents the descriptive text included in publications about the standards. This text offers an overview and discussion

32 • Instructor Competencies

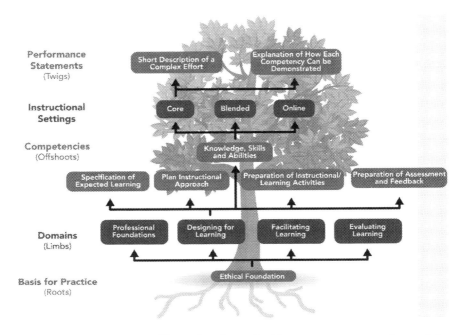

Figure 2.2 Tree structure illustrating the revised instructor competencies model.

of each of the competencies along with a description of the performance statements.

Drafting the Updated Competencies

As the result of numerous iterations, the new model was applied to better conceptualize and illustrate the different instructor skills/competencies needed depending on an instructional setting. IBSTPI's competencies provide a standard set of KSAs needed by effective instructors across a range of settings and instructional approaches; the model needed to clearly delineate an instructor's skills independent of setting and organization. Much discussion ensued to reach a consensus on the terms to use in defining these roles, but the roles themselves were not vigorously debated. Because the Foundation domain assumes expected competence in the instructor duties independent of the specific domains (e.g., online) of the instructor responsibility, these competencies are seen as core. In today's instructional settings, emerging technologies such as those that promote virtual collaborations, are ever present. In many respects, instructors need to possess TPACK to know about existing capabilities of technologies as well as know how to adapt instruction to use these technologies effectively. What term best describes an instructor who integrates technologies and tools into their teaching but who does not necessarily use a specific type of technology, for example? Keeping in mind that IBSTPI standards are "technology agnostic" and are not based on instructional trends, it was decided that the term *blended* best describes an instructor who selectively blends tools and technologies into instructional practices and contexts. Ultimately, the model was adapted to include *three* conditions (strands) that define instructors' work, and thereby the competencies required to perform that work. See Table 2.1.

The team tested the model by converting several of the current competency statements and their associated performance statements into the model. This process led to clarity and deeper thinking about what should be considered general competencies for all instructors and how to determine which revised or new statements were required to fully describe competent instructors in the blended and online instructor environments. During this involved stage of work, efforts focused on updating the competencies and performance statements to both refresh to current (and hopefully long-term future) terminology and to better describe competence for multiple audiences in the global community of instructor practitioners. It became evident that some of the competencies needed to be updated, some might need to be deleted, and several could be retained as stated. The team questioned if they should reorganize the competencies and discussed the need to write new performance statements that are practical and clearly communicate.

Each team member picked a competency of interest and presented the competency and performance statement in the format of the model. We had to address how an instructor can demonstrate the competency and we had to determine the unique aspects to blended and online learning settings. For example, when an instructor is demonstrating effective questioning skills, how does an instructor adapt the types of questions? Rigorous discussions followed, and it was concluded that the model was working to present the competencies in a way that identifies general competencies for all instructors and additional sets of competencies for those who work in

TABLE 2.1 Strands of Instructor Environments

CORE suggests that *all* instructors should have these instructionally foundational competencies
BLENDED suggests that any instructor should have these competencies if using digital technologies and tools to support instruction (e.g., presentation tools, course management programs, etc.) and learning (e.g., clickers, online quizzes, etc.)
ONLINE suggests that any instructor should have these competencies if instructing entirely online

different types of environments. The modification process was guided by these three primary questions:

- What competencies does an instructor require to work effectively in a particular learning setting (foundational, blended, or online)?
- For each competency, what does an instructor do to exhibit the competency?
- How can each performance statement be demonstrated?

With the 2004 standards in hand, the team closely examined and discussed each of the evaluation competencies. This process led to a quest for more information. Specifically, there was a need to locate literature and empirical evidence indicating the best practices, strategies, and tools for instructors to effectively evaluate. In the years since the 2004 instructor competencies publication, a greater emphasis has been placed on learning and not on instruction—an emphasis generally referred to as "learner-centered" or "student-centered." What exactly is meant by these terms varies in the literature due to the notion that a "shape shifting concept defies easy definition" (Schweisfurth, 2013, p. 136). Still, there is an understanding that the shift to a learner-centered approach requires rethinking instructor and learner roles and the recognition that an instructor's role is to provide the conditions for learning. In an attempt to address this lack of definitional consistency, Bremner (2021) conducted a meta-analysis of learner-centered and student-centered journal articles that led to the identification of a flexible 6- or 10-aspect framework for defining these concepts. The aspects include, for example, active learning, adapting to needs, and formative assessment. The 2004 instructor competencies reflect a time when learning was viewed as a product; today, it is primarily viewed as a process. When learning is viewed as a process instead of a product, summative assessment to monitor learning is insufficient and needs to be integrated with formative assessment for learning. Thus, the 2022 competencies now include a competency to prepare assessment and feedback as well as an additional competency to evaluate instructional effectiveness. A distinction between assessment and evaluation was needed to illustrate their distinctive functions and to provide relevant performance statements.

The team members divided responsibility for the initial review and writing of performance statements. Once a draft version of the evaluation competency performance statements was completed, the team then modified, shifted, added, or deleted performance statements. During extensive discussions, SME reviews, and revisions of the evaluation performance statements, it became apparent that evaluation is not something that is just done to instructors, but rather they are tasked with an active role in planning, gathering, and learning from evaluation efforts.

During this intensive and iterative drafting phase, the statements were analyzed, debated, and rewritten, based on input from the IBSTPI board members and other experts from across the globe. This effort ensured consistency of format, language, and clarity, and once it was completed, the new competencies were deemed ready for the validation process.

Validating the Competencies

In the years since 2004, online survey tools have become more powerful in facilitating survey research and its analysis. After much discussion and review, the team decided to use an online survey tool that was designed for researchers because of its enhanced survey features allowing for block-based questionnaire design and logical branching options. Because the instructor competencies contain 150 evidence-based performance statements within 19 competencies organized into four domains by core, online, and blended instructional environments, it was important to use a survey tool that allowed for skip logic (i.e., the feature that allows for participants to skip questions) and for display logic (i.e., the feature that allows for participants to answer a unique version of the survey that is based on their responses). The validation survey is distributed internationally, and we wanted the ability to translate the survey into multiple languages. With these features in mind, we selected Qualtrics as our survey tool and then developed and pilot-tested our survey. In addition to English, the survey was translated into Arabic, Chinese, Japanese, Russian, and Spanish.

To obtain a large sample of instructors from across the globe, the online survey was distributed using a snowball sampling technique across various social media platforms, groups, listservs, and the IBSTPI website to a wide network of instructors. The survey instrument asked respondents to review the competencies and performance statements and then rate the criticality of those statements according to the following scale: *not critical* = 1, *slightly critical* = 2, *moderately critical* = 3, *critical* = 4, *highly critical* = 5. All of the participants were to rank the core performance statements; those with experience in blended settings also ranked the blended performance statements, and those with online instruction experience ranked the online performance statements. Chapter 4 details the validation study and provides specifics on the respondents, data analysis methods, and the findings.

CONCLUSION

The IBSTPI competency model, based on job roles, is designed to link together competencies, job role, and performance indicators. This competency development model, recognized in the field for being comprehensive and specific, was applied to revise and update the 2004 instructor competencies. The competency modeling systematic process, informed by current pedagogical evidence-based findings, new technologies and contexts, expert reviews, iterative revisions, and a validation process, resulted in the fourth iteration of the instructor competencies. By using this development model, we identified the core competencies needed for all instructors, as well as those for blended and online settings.

REFERENCES

Arifin, M. A., Rasdi, R. M., Anuar, M. A. M., & Omar, M. K. (2017). Addressing competency gaps for vocational instructor through competency modelling. *International Journal of Academic Research in Business and Social Sciences, 7*(4), 1201–1216. https://doi.org/10.6007/IJARBSS/v7-i4/2970

Beaudoin, M., Jung, I., Suzuki, K., Kutz, G., & Grabowski, B. (2013). *Online learner competencies: Knowledge, skills, and attitudes for successful learning in online and blended settings.* Information Age Publishing.

Boyatzis, R. (2009). Competencies as a behavioral approach to emotional intelligence. *Journal of Management Development, 28*(9), 749–770. https://doi.org/10.1108/02621710910987647

Brantley-Dias, L., Kinuthia, W., Shoffner, M., de Castro, C., & Rigole, N. (2007). Developing pedagogical technology integration content knowledge in preservice teachers: A case study approach. *Journal of Computing in Teacher Education, 23*(4), 143–150. https://doi.org/10.1108/02621710910987647

Bremner, N. (2021). The multiple meanings of "student-centered" or "learner-centered" education, and the case for a more flexible approach to defining it. *Comparative Education, 57*(2), 159–186. https://doi.org/10.1080/03050068.2020.1805863

Drisko, J. (2014). Competencies and their assessment. *Journal of Social Work Education, 50*(3), 414–426. https://doi.org/10.1080/10437797.2014.917927

Epstein, R., & Hundert, E. (2002). Defining and assessing professional competence. *Journal of the American Medical Association, 287*(2), 226–235. https://doi.org/10.1001/jama.287.2.226

Fink, A. A. (2017). The case for competencies. *HR Magazine, 62*(4), 22–23. https://www.proquest.com/docview/1895911270?accountid=13158&parentSessionId=iZjA8f9LGnJ7CeVJObQ4sQwNticxOtjC1YzMCX56UjM%3D&pq-origsite=summon

Foxon, M., Richey, R., Roberts, R., & Spannus, T. (2003). *Training manager competencies: The standards* (3rd ed.). ERIC Clearinghouse on Information and Technology.

Klein, J. D., Spector, J. M., Grabowski, B., & de la Teja, E. (2004). *Instructor competencies: Standards for face-to-face, online, and blended settings.* Information Age Publishing.

Koszalka, T., Russ-Eft, D., & Reiser, R. (2013). *Instructional designer competencies: The standards* (4th ed.). Information Age Publishing.

Kunter, M., Klusmann, U., Baumert, J., Richter, D., Voss, T., & Hachfeld, A. (2013). Professional competence of teachers: Effects on instructional quality and student development. *Journal of Educational Psychology, 105*(3), 805–820. https://doi.org/10.1037/a0032583

McClelland, D. (1973). Testing for competence rather than for "intelligence." *The American Psychologist, 28*(1), 1–14. https://doi.org/10.1037/h0034092

Megahed, N. (2018). A critical review of the literature and practice of competency modelling. *KnE Social Sciences, 3*(10), 104–126. https://doi.org/10.18502/kss.v3i10.3106

Mishra, P., & Koehler, M. (2007). Technological pedagogical content knowledge (TPCK): Confronting the wicked problems of teaching with technology. In C. Crawford et al. (Eds.), *Proceedings of Society for Information Technology and Teacher Education International Conference 2007* (pp. 2214–2226). AACE.

Polly, D., Mims, C., Shepherd, C. E., & Inan, F. (2010). Evidence of impact: Transforming teacher education with preparing tomorrow's teachers to teach with technology (PT3) grants. *Teaching and Teacher Education, 26*, 863–870. https://doi.org/10.1016/j.tate.2009.10.024

Russ-Eft, D., Bober-Michel, M., Koszalka, T., & Sleezer, C. (2014). *Fieldbook of IBSTPI evaluator competencies*. Information Age Publishing.

Salman, M., Ganie, S., & Saleem, I. (2020). The concept of competence: A thematic review and discussion. *European Journal of Training and Development, 44*(6–7), 717–742. https://doi.org/10.1108/EJTD-10-2019-0171

Sampson, D., & Fytros, D. (2008). Competence models in technology-enhanced competence-based learning. In H. H. Adelsberger, Kinshuk, B. Collis, & J. M. Pawlowski, & Sampson, D. G. (Eds.). *Handbook on information technologies for education and training* (2nd ed.; pp. 155–178). Springer.

Sanghi, S. (2016). *The handbook of competency mapping: Understanding, designing and implementing competency models in organizations* (3rd ed.). SAGE.

Schweisfurth, M. (2013). *Learner-centred education in international perspective: Whose pedagogy for whose development?* Routledge.

Shippmann, J. S., Ash, R. A., Batjtsta, M., Carr, L., Eyde, L. D., Hesketh, B., Kehoe, J., Pearlman, K., Prien, E. P., & Sanchez, J. I. (2000). The practice of competency modeling. *Personnel Psychology, 53*(3), 703–740. https://doi.org/10.1111/j.1744-6570.2000.tb00220.x

Shulman, L. (1986). Those who understand: Knowledge growth in teaching. *Educational Researcher, 15*(2), 4–14. https://doi.org/10.3102/0013189X015002004

Staskevica, A. (2019). The importance of competency model development. *Acta Oeconomica Pragensia, 27*(2), 62–71. https://doi.org/10.18267/j.aop.622

Thompson, K., Reichin, S., McClure, J., Loftis, M., & Frame, M. (2017, October 28). *Defending your competency model: Sit back, relax and get comfortable* [Conference session]. 13th Annual River Cities Industrial and Organizational Psychology Conference, Chattanooga, TN, United States. https://scholar.utc.edu/rcio/2017/sessions/22/

Vazirani, N. (2010). Competencies and competency model—A brief overview of its development and application. *SIES Journal of Management, 7*(1), 121–131. https://api.semanticscholar.org/CorpusID:14211611

CHAPTER 3

LITERATURE REVIEW OF INSTRUCTOR COMPETENCIES

CHAPTER OVERVIEW

While the previous chapters explain the importance of instructor competencies, this chapter examines the existing research on instructor competencies. In this literature review, we use the terms *instructor* or *faculty* synonymously and *students* or *learners* interchangeably to maintain the original terminology used by the researchers. Reviewing research on instructor competencies provides readers guidance on the competencies instructors need to have to be effective in their teaching. This review of research also shows that the IBSTPI instructor competencies are grounded in research. The goal of this chapter is to review research on instructor competencies in the four domains that are critical for instructors in their teaching (a) Foundations, (b) Design, (c) Facilitation, and (d) Evaluation.

Orienting Questions

- What foundational competencies are essential for instructors in their teaching?
- What design competencies are essential for instructors in their teaching?

> - What facilitation competencies are essential for instructors in their teaching?
> - What evaluation competencies are essential for instructors in their teaching?

Research on performance capabilities of instructors by studying competencies dates back to the 1970s. Canfield (1972) defines competency statements as "descriptions of abilities, knowledge, and attitudes thought to be needed by or characteristic of persons holding the positions or doing the work toward which the educational experience is directed" (p. 1). There were several studies in the 1970s and 1980s examining competencies for instructors for effective teaching. Some of the earlier research on instructor competencies has focused on discipline- or subject-specific instructor competencies. For instance, Canfield (1972) examined competencies for allied health instructors, Parr (1976) studied competencies for first-year band instructors, and Blank (1979) studied professional education competencies for community college technical instructors. Dickens (1980) identified 113 specific competencies in eight categories for developmental educators. These included (a) manifest personal qualities, (b) application of interpersonal skills, (c) ability to structure and sequence skill competencies, (d) instructional planning skills, (e) instructional delivery (i.e., teaching), (f) assessment of student progress, (g) public relations, and (h) program administration. McGroarty (1985) examined competencies for bilingual vocational training instructors and determined that language proficiency, technical skills, and vocational awareness were essential for them to be effective. Ryan (1987) examined instructor competencies for fieldwork supervision of occupational therapy and physical therapy students. Instructors are first and foremost content experts but in addition, they have to be competent in other domains related to teaching.

The International Board of Standards for Training, Performance, and Instruction published the first volume of the book on instructor competencies in 1988 and validated in 1993 (IBSTPI, 1993). The second version of the IBSTPI instructor competencies categorized competencies into professional domain, preparation and planning, instructional methods and strategies, assessment and evaluation, and management (Klein et al., 2004). Building on the prior IBSTPI competencies, the current instructor competencies are categorized into four domains: Foundations, Design, Facilitation, and Evaluation (see Figure 3.1). The IBSTPI competencies were designed based on research findings and expert instructor feedback. The literature on instructor competencies reviews each of these four competency domains in the following section.

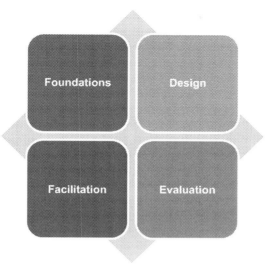

Figure 3.1 IBSTPI instructor competency domains.

FOUNDATIONS

Foundational competencies show that instructors are members of a profession with responsibilities beyond teaching and learning (Klein et al., 2004). The Foundations domain provides expected instructor competence regardless of the specific domains of instructor responsibility and should be in practice across all domains. In the IBSTPI second edition of instructor competencies, these competencies were labeled professional competencies and included communicating effectively, updating and improving one's professional knowledge and skills, complying with established ethical and legal standards, and establishing and maintaining professional credibility (Klein et al., 2004). In the IBSTPI third edition, these key competencies are now referred to with a more representative name as foundational competencies and include six competencies shown.

FOUNDATIONAL COMPETENCIES

1. Communicate effectively.
2. Improve instructor practices.
3. Respond to situational factors that may impact learning and performance.
4. Comply with ethical and legal standards.
5. Establish and maintain professionalism.
6. Manage instructional resources.

Communication is the process of imparting information, and instructors' ability to communicate effectively is an important foundational competency as teaching relies on communication aspects such as lecturing, listening, and providing feedback. Among the competencies that Sali-ot (2011) examined with instructors and students in the Philippines, communication with learners was rated the highest. The competencies they examined under communication included listening skills, a positive attitude towards teaching, providing feedback to learners, giving clear directions, and using questions that lead students to analyze, synthesize, and think critically. Yıldırım (2021), when researching attitudes and self-efficacy of student teachers, found that the communication skills of the instructors affected the attitudes and self-efficacy beliefs of student teachers towards the teaching profession. Their findings demonstrate that instructors' communication skills also affect their students' attitudes and self-efficacy beliefs. Valiee et al. (2016) highlighted that clinical instructors' most effective teaching strategy for nursing students was "treating students, clients, and colleagues with respect" (p. 259), and this helped to improve students' motivation for learning. Also, instructors need to keep the cultural differences of their students in mind during communication (Chen & Starosta, 1996).

Research has also been conducted on foundational competencies in online teaching. Davidson (2019) surveyed 500 students on their perspective of future online faculty competencies in an online setting. The survey findings revealed that faculty communication, technical and computer competencies especially using visual, auditory, and other multimedia tools are important. The survey results also found that it is important for faculty to be patient with students while students experience different issues, and to be flexible with class requirements, schedules, and communication modalities. Similarly, Martin, Budhrani, and Wang (2019) examined readiness competencies for online instructors and identified communication as one of the categories, with others being design, technical aspects, and time management. Some of the communication competencies they identified included sending periodic announcements, responding promptly to questions, using synchronous and asynchronous communication methods, and promptly providing feedback.

Sali-ot (2011) also discussed competencies on professional standards, which included acting as an appropriate model in terms of ethics, attitudes, and values; understanding and following school policies; procedures and their effects including professional standards; showing evidence of cooperation with others in planning and teaching; and accepting responsibility with enthusiasm. Sims and Falkenberg (2013) studied the role of education for sustainable development in undergraduate and graduate teacher education programs in Canada. Their findings suggest the importance of experiential, interdisciplinary, and inter-institutional learning, problem-based learning around real-life issues within the community and the natural environment, and building partnerships with colleagues, students, and community organizations. Alexander et al. (2012) found several competencies necessary for meaningful student learning in addition to finding subject matter expertise essential. These competencies included authentic activities and multiple instructional delivery models, multiple ways of assessing student learning, and skills necessary outside the classroom. Participants also emphasized interpersonal and affective components of effective teaching.

Instructors, while working alone in some situations, also collaborate—with peers, by seeking and sharing input, and with instructional designers to design courses and instructional resources (Brown et al., 2013; Chen & Carliner, 2021). Establishing and maintaining professionalism in their behavior and attitudes is a necessary competency for instructors. They also have to be competent in using emerging technologies (Lewis et al., 2013; Martin, Kumar, & She, 2021). Finally, managing instructional resources is an essential foundational competency for instructors. The instructional resources could include using various tools, maintaining security and privacy of student data, and managing versions of instructional material.

DESIGN

Design is the process an instructor goes through to plan out the various aspects of the course, including lessons, resources, activities to achieve the student learning objectives, and quality experiences. This includes identifying course goals and objectives, planning instructional and learning strategies, creating instructional materials, preparing instructional and learning activities for students to engage in the learning process, and designing assessments and opportunities to provide feedback.

DESIGN COMPETENCIES

7. Specify expected learning.
8. Plan instructional and learning approach.
9. Plan instructional resources.
10. Prepare for instructional and learning activities.
11. Prepare assessment and feedback.

As part of the design competencies, instructors specify the learning expectation for the students. Instructional design models recommend that instructors include measurable goals and objectives during designing instructors. While goals are broad generalized statements of what the learner will achieve at the end of the course, objectives are more specific, measurable, short-term, observable student behaviors and can be achieved in the various units, lessons, or modules (Martin, 2011). Ausubel (1968) emphasized that stating an objective at the beginning of the instruction assists the learners in structuring their learning. After the identification of objectives, it is important to sequence them to maximize student learning. Another critical aspect of design that instructors need to be competent in is maintaining the instructional alignment between goals, objectives, activities, and assessments (Martin, 2011). Based on the Dick and Carey instructional model, designers create assessments before the instructional material to stay aligned with the goals and objectives (Dick et al., 2013).

Instructors select learning strategies for their students based on the learning tasks and various delivery methods. While there are various classifications of instructional strategies, some of them include direct instruction, interactive instruction, individual study, experiential instruction, and indirect instruction (Gregory & Chapman, 2012; Moore, 2014; Saskatchewan Education Department, 1991), instructor-focused instructional strategies; learner-focused instructional strategies; problem-solving sample event; discussion-brainstorming; modeling, simulation, role taking; thinking, interrogating, interpreting; presentation; question-answer; writing, summarizing, note-taking; and research-project (Eristi & Akdeniz, 2012). Sali-ot (2011) identified instructional strategies and techniques including instructors developing and demonstrating problem-solving skills; using a variety of instructional strategies, resources, and materials; structuring the use of time to facilitate student learning; providing learning experiences to enable students to transfer learning; and demonstrating knowledge of the subject matter. There are some strategies that are specific to online and blended courses, such as asynchronous discussion facilitation, providing feedback through various modalities (e.g., audio, video, text), using instructor-generated video, hosting synchronous discussions, and so on (Bolliger & Martin, 2021).

Planning for instructional resources is another design competency expected of instructors. While instructors can create some instructional materials, they are also able to use or modify existing instructional resources. Mehmet and colleagues (2018), on interviewing and observing instructors, identified roles and competencies in distance education. Similarly, Martin, Budhrani, Kumar, and Ritzhaupt (2019), on interviewing award-winning online instructors, identified material development and course design skills as critical skills for online instructors. Sali-ot (2011) categorized design competencies to include planning teaching materials. Some competencies in this category included planning units of instruction in various ways, using information about the effectiveness of instruction, keeping informed of current trends and resources available, planning expectations for the learning process and student readiness, and using appropriate instructional materials. Preparing instructional and learning activities is another integral design competency for instructors.

Creating assessments is an essential competency in design for instructors. In the online course design elements rubric that Martin, Bolliger, and Flowers (2021) created, they included the importance of assessments aligned with learning objectives, including formative assessments and summative assessments. While formative assessments assist in providing feedback on learner progress, summative assessments measure student learning. It is also helpful to include a variety of assessments and for these to occur throughout the course. Award-winning online instructors emphasized the importance of integrating a variety of course assessments and using both traditional and authentic assessments to evaluate their learners. They also recommended using rubrics to set clear expectations and grade projects and assignments (Martin, Budhrani, Kumar, & Ritzhaupt, 2019).

FACILITATION

Facilitation is the process of supporting learners to acquire knowledge and skills and actively participate in the course. In this chapter, we use the term *facilitation* instead of *teaching* or *instruction*, to make the term broader. In addition to being classroom teachers, instructors can also be teaching or facilitating in various settings, facilitating the learning process. Martin et al. (2018), when researching facilitation strategies, described a facilitator as one who guides the learning process and constantly monitors the activities, being readily available to provide support to the students. Phelps and Vlachopoulos (2020) examined competencies for entry-level facilitators of synchronous distance education. When interviewing instructors, they found that an entry-level facilitator must possess technical/operational, classroom management, communication, and design/delivery competencies and foster learner success in a synchronous virtual environment. Leighton et al. (2018) validated the facilitator competency rubric, which included preparation, prebriefing, facilitation, debriefing, and evaluation as the constructs.

FACILITATION COMPETENCIES

12. Engage learners.
13. Adapt instruction to learners and learning environment.
14. Promote learning through feedback.
15. Promote retention of knowledge, skills, and attitudes.
16. Promote the transfer of learned knowledge, skills, and attitudes to other contexts.
17. Apply classroom management principles.

Irrespective of the delivery method of the instruction, engaging and motivating the learner is a vital facilitation competency for the instructor. Student engagement is defined as "the student's psychological investment in an effort directed toward learning, understanding, or mastering the knowledge, skills, or crafts that academic work is intended to promote" (Newmann et al., 1992, p. 12). Instructors have to be competent to facilitate the active involvement of the learner in the learning process. Research has examined various dimensions of engagement (e.g., cognitive, emotional, behavioral) and environmental factors that contribute to engagement (e.g., peer engagement, collaborative engagement, multimodal engagement). Engaging the learner who is at a distance might be even more challenging but nonetheless very important. There are various evidence-based strategies instructors can use to engage the learners (Bolliger & Martin, 2021).

Meeting the needs of the learners by adapting instruction to learners and the learner environment is another essential instructor facilitation competency. Lalley and Gentile (2008) note the need for instructors to adapt instruction to learners' prior knowledge. Alhassan and Abosi (2014) found that teachers have limited to moderate competence in adaptive instruction, and adaptive teaching and competence are strongly associated. They define adaptive instruction as "a way and form to respond to differentiating learning needs of learners during instruction" (p. 3). They recommend that teachers be trained to set up alternative instructional goals, adapt curriculum content and delivery systems, and use specific instructional procedures based on certain student characteristics and develop skills to identify students' learning needs.

Practice and feedback are essential in the learning cycle, and competent instructors are able to effectively and efficiently design practice opportunities and provide feedback. Gagné (1985) notes the importance of providing opportunities for students to practice in order to master the objective after the presentation of instructional material. Deliberate practice focusing on a reasonable yet challenging goal improves student learning and performance (Ericsson et al., 1993). Providing feedback on learners' performance assists them in strengthening their knowledge of correct information and reduces the incorrect information they have processed during instruction (Kulhavy et al., 1979). Martin et al. (2018), when examining facilitation strategies, found that timely response to student questions and timely feedback were the two most helpful strategies to online students. It is necessary, however, to consider the appropriate timing of feedback and recognize that there is a body of literature demonstrating that delayed feedback can support learning (Mullet et al., 2014). Competent instructors are able to identify how soon and how often feedback is needed for learning. Additionally, providing feedback using various modalities is also helpful for the learners.

As Gagné (1985) described in a discussion of the nine events of instruction, two crucial events of instruction are promoting retention and transfer. When testing simulation-based training, Cheung et al. (2018) recommended that integrated instruction may improve trainees' skill retention and transfer. Chariker et al. (2011) concluded that computer-based learning with adaptive exploration supported efficient learning, good long-term retention, and successful transfer to the interpretation of biomedical images in neuroanatomy instruction.

Applying classroom management is another essential facilitation competency for instructors. Classroom management includes setting ground rules, employing time management, maintaining a positive learning climate, and resolving conflicts and problems. A study by Akbari Lakeh et al. (2012) found that the most powerful competency was classroom management. Korpershoek et al. (2016), in a meta-analysis on classroom management in primary education, found that including classroom management strategies had a small but significant effect on students' academic, behavioral, and emotional outcomes. Time management is a challenge when instructors teach online, but Oyarzun et al. (2020) recommend various strategies to manage their time. Overall, effective facilitation is an essential competency for instructors.

EVALUATION

Evaluation is a critical competency for instructors to judge the value of the instruction. Patton et al. (2016) sought to actively engage faculty in becoming familiar with a variety of assessment methods, along with their appropriateness for evaluating instruction. The IBSTPI competencies differentiate the terms *assessment* and *evaluation*. While assessment focuses on measuring learning, evaluation focuses on measuring instruction. Martin, Budhrani, Kumar, and Ritzhaupt (2019), on interviewing award-winning online instructors, found instructors assumed the role of assessor and evaluator in their courses. The award-winning instructors highlighted the importance of participating in a quality assurance process to get feedback on the course, as well as receiving both student and peer feedback to improve the course.

EVALUATION COMPETENCIES

18. Plan and prepare for monitoring and evaluating instruction.
19. Evaluate instructional effectiveness.

While it is common for universities to have a systematic evaluation method to collect feedback from students, it is also important to include other data collection opportunities from peers, administrators, and employers. As part of the process, it is helpful to plan the evaluation and manage the evaluation data collection. Berk (2018) suggests 15 strategies for measuring teaching effectiveness and recommends including multiple sources of evaluation. These include evaluation instruments from students, instructors, peers, faculty, administrators, and employers. Student evaluation strategies include student end-of-course ratings, student midterm feedback, student exit and alumni ratings, and student outcome measures. Instructor evaluation includes self-ratings, teaching scholarship, and teaching awards. Peer evaluation strategies include peer classroom observations, peer review of course materials, external expert ratings, mentors' advice, video classroom review, and teaching/course portfolio review. Administrative evaluation strategies include administrator ratings, and employer evaluation includes employer ratings.

Tobin et al. (2015) recommend six target aspects of evaluation—including university resources, curriculum, course, student learning, student satisfaction, and teaching—and also emphasize the importance of collecting learning analytics from learning management systems for evaluating online courses. This shows both student performance as well as instructor presence in the courses. Several institutions have a quality assurance process for the teaching process (Ellis & Hogard, 2018). The Quality Matters review process is an example of a quality assurance process to provide feedback on course design (Lowenthal & Hodges, 2015). It has specific rubrics for higher education, K–12 education, and continuing education. The quality assurance process is helpful before the course is taught.

In a meta-analysis, Uttl and colleagues (2017) concluded that student evaluation of teaching is not related to student learning and may not provide much detail on teacher effectiveness. However, student evaluation of teaching provides instructors with feedback on various aspects of the teaching and learning process (Bush et al., 2018). Debroy et al. (2019) recommend using student evaluation of teaching as a tool for faculty development and quality assurance in medical education.

Some institutions have peer observation of the teaching process in place to measure teaching effectiveness (Donnelly, 2007). Hammersley-Fletcher and Orsmond (2004) suggest that peer observation of teaching can be used both in formative and summative processes where one focuses on improvement whereas the other focuses on accountability. When meaningful feedback is provided for new instructors through peer observations, it helps them to strengthen their teaching practices.

Thomas and Graham (2019) analyzed evaluation rubrics for online teaching to identify the most observable teaching behaviors. They concluded with three recommendations: Online instructor evaluation should include course observations with instructor behaviors; observational rubrics should include items that focus on building relationships and community among students; and a comprehensive model of online teaching competencies should be included in observational rubrics.

RESEARCH METHODS USED TO STUDY INSTRUCTOR COMPETENCIES

Instructor competencies are studied using various research approaches. Research has been conducted using quantitative and qualitative methods by interviewing expert and novice instructors, observing instructors and courses, and surveying students for their perceptions on competencies for effective teaching. Senemoglu et al. (2016) conducted in-depth interviews with graduate students for their opinion about graduate educators' competencies. Their study categorized instructor competencies as subject area knowledge, facilitating learning, advisement, measurement and evaluation, communication, and expectations. Sali-ot (2011) used a questionnaire and examined five categories of competencies: planning teaching materials, instructional strategies and techniques, communications with learners, learner reinforcement involvement, and professional standards.

COMPETENCIES TO TEACH IN DIFFERENT DELIVERY METHODS

With instructors teaching in different delivery methods including face-to-face, web-enhanced, blended/hybrid, and online settings, instructors need to be competent to teach in these various instructional settings. Several researchers have examined competencies for blended and online settings. Pulham et al. (2018) examined the competencies required for K–12 instructors to teach in blended and online settings. Archibald et al. (2021) validated a blended teaching readiness instrument, while Martin, Budhrani, Kumar, and Ritzhaupt (2019) validated an online teaching readiness instrument. These include readiness competencies for various contexts. The COVID-19 pandemic has shown the need for instructor preparation to teach in online and blended settings. Instructors who were prepared to teach in online and blended settings had an easier transition to online teaching during COVID-19 compared to those who did not. Research emphasizes the need for professional development for instructors to teach in online and blended settings (Lockee, 2021).

SUMMARY

This chapter introduces the research on instructor competencies and discusses them through the four domains of Foundations, Design, Facilitation, and Evaluation. Instructors are expected to have a number of foundational competencies, including communication, collaboration, response to situational factors, ethical and legal compliance, professionalism, and management of instructional resources. In the design domain, the competencies specify expected learning including: setting goals and objectives, ensuring instructional alignment, planning instructional and learning approaches and instructional resources, preparing instructional and learning activities, and preparing assessment with feedback. In the facilitation domain, instructors demonstrate competencies to engage learners; adapt instruction; provide feedback; promote retention and transfer of knowledge, skills, and attitudes; and apply classroom management principles. Finally, in the evaluation domain, they demonstrate competencies in evaluating instruction, and instructional effectiveness.

REFERENCES

Akbari Lakeh, M., Karimi Moonaghi, H., & Makarem, A. (2012). Medical faculty members' teaching competencies and factors affecting it. *Future of Medical Education Journal, 2*(3), 7–10. https://journals.mums.ac.ir/article_342.html

Alexander, A., Karvonen, M., Ulrich, J., Davis, T., & Wade, A. (2012). Community college faculty competencies. *Community College Journal of Research and Practice, 36*(11), 849–862. https://eric.ed.gov/?id=EJ977882

Alhassan, A.-R. K., & Abosi, O. C. (2014). Teacher effectiveness in adapting instruction to the needs of pupils with learning difficulties in regular primary schools in Ghana. *SAGE Open, 4*(1). https://doi.org/10.1177/2158244013518929

Archibald, D. E., Graham, C. R., & Larsen, R. (2021). Validating a blended teaching readiness instrument for primary/secondary preservice teachers. *British Journal of Educational Technology, 52*(2), 536–551. https://doi.org/10.1111/bjet.13060

Ausubel, D. P. (1968). Facilitating meaningful verbal learning in the classroom. *The Arithmetic Teacher, 15*(2), 126–132. https://doi.org/10.5951/AT.15.2.0126

Berk, R. A. (2018). Start spreading the news: Use multiple sources of evidence to evaluate teaching. *The Journal of Faculty Development, 32*(1), 73–81. https://eric.ed.gov/?id=EJ1167647

Blank, W. E. (1979). Analysis of professional competencies important to community college technical instructors: Implications for CBTE. *Journal of Industrial Teacher Education, 16*(2), 56–69. https://eric.ed.gov/?id=EJ202660

Bolliger, D., & Martin, F. (2021). Factors underlying the perceived importance of online student engagement strategies. *Journal of Applied Research in Higher Education, 13*(2), 404–419. https://doi.org/10.1108/JARHE-02-2020-0045

Brown, B., Eaton, S., Jacobsen, D., Roy, S., & Friesen, S. (2013). Instructional design collaboration: A professional learning and growth experience. *Journal of Online Learning and Teaching, 9*(3), 439. http://hdl.handle.net/1880/109272

Bush, M. A., Rushton, S., Conklin, J. L., & Oermann, M. H. (2018). Considerations for developing a student evaluation of teaching form. *Teaching and Learning in Nursing, 13*(2), 125–128. https://doi.org/10.1016/j.teln.2017.10.002

Canfield, A. A. (1972). *Competencies for allied health instructors.* Florida University. Center for Allied Health Instructional Personnel. https://files.eric.ed.gov/fulltext/ED074258.pdf

Chariker, J. H., Naaz, F., & Pani, J. R. (2011). Computer-based learning of neuroanatomy: A longitudinal study of learning, transfer, and retention. *Journal of Educational Psychology, 103*(1), 19. https://doi.org/10.1037/a0021680

Chen, G. M., & Starosta, W. J. (1996). Intercultural communication competence: A synthesis. *Annals of the International Communication Association, 19*(1), 353–383. https://doi.org/10.1080/23808985.1996.11678935

Chen, Y., & Carliner, S. (2021). A special SME: An integrative literature review of the relationship between instructional designers and faculty in the design of online courses for higher education. *Performance Improvement Quarterly, 33*(4), 471–495. https://doi.org/10.1002/piq.21339

Cheung, J. J., Kulasegaram, K. M., Woods, N. N., Moulton, C. A., Ringsted, C. V., & Brydges, R. (2018). Knowing how and knowing why: Testing the effect of instruction designed for cognitive integration on procedural skills transfer. *Advances in Health Sciences Education, 23*(1), 61–74. https://doi.org/10.1007/s10459-017-9774-1

Davidson, P. (2019). Future online faculty competencies: Student perspectives. *International Journal on E-Learning, 18*(3), 233–250. https://eric.ed.gov/?id=EJ1218532

Debroy, A., Ingole, A., & Mudey, A. (2019). Teachers' perceptions on student evaluation of teaching as a tool for faculty development and quality assurance in medical education. *Journal of Education and Health Promotion, 8*(1), 218. https://www.ncbi.nlm.nih.gov/pmc/articles/PMC6905290/

Dick, W., Carey, L., & Carey, J. O. (2013). A model for the systematic design of instruction. In R. D. Tennyson, F. Schott, N. M. Seel, & S. Dijkstra (Eds.), *Instructional design: International perspectives: Theory, research, and models* (pp. 361–370). Routledge.

Dickens, M. E. (1980). *Competencies for developmental educators.* Tri-County Technical College Report. https://eric.ed.gov/?id=ED203909

Donnelly, R. (2007). Perceived impact of peer observation of teaching in higher education. *International Journal of Teaching and Learning in Higher Education, 19*(2), 117–129. https://www.researchgate.net/publication/255016853

Ellis, R., & Hogard, E. (Eds.). (2018). *Handbook of quality assurance for university teaching.* Routledge.

Ericsson, K., Krampe, R., & Tescher-Romer, C. (1993). The role of deliberate practice in the acquisition of expert performance. *Psychological Review, 100*(3), 363–406. https://doi.org10.1037//0033-295X.100.3.363

Eristi, B., & Akdeniz, C. (2012). Development of a scale to diagnose instructional strategies. *Contemporary Educational Technology, 3*(2), 141–161. https://doi.org/10.30935/cedtech/6074

Gagné, R. (1985). *The conditions of learning and theory of instruction*. Wadsworth.

Gregory, G. H., & Chapman, C. (2012). *Differentiated instructional strategies: One size doesn't fit all*. Corwin.

Hammersley-Fletcher, L., & Orsmond, P. (2004). Evaluating our peers: Is peer observation a meaningful process? *Studies in Higher Education, 29*(4), 489–503. https://doi.org/10.1080/0307507042000236380

IBSTPI. (1993). *Instructor competencies: The standards* (Vol. 1). International Board of Standards for Training, Performance and Instruction.

Klein, J. D., Spector, J. M., Grabowski, B. L., & de la Teja, I. (2004). *Instructor competencies: Standards for face-to-face, online, and blended settings*. Information Age Publishing.

Korpershoek, H., Harms, T., de Boer, H., van Kuijk, M., & Doolaard, S. (2016). A meta-analysis of the effects of classroom management strategies and classroom management programs on students' academic, behavioral, emotional, and motivational outcomes. *Review of Educational Research, 86*(3), 643–680. https://doi.org/10.3102/0034654315626799

Kulhavy, R. W., Yekovich, F. R., & Dyer, J. W. (1979). Feedback and content review in programmed instruction. *Contemporary Educational Psychology, 4,* 91–98. https://doi.org/10.1016/0361-476X(79)90062-6

Lalley, J. P., & Gentile, J. R. (2008). Adapting instruction to individuals: Based on the evidence, what should it mean? *International Journal of Teaching and Learning in Higher Education, 20*(3), 462–475. https://eric.ed.gov/?id=EJ869330

Leighton, K., Mudra, V., & Gilbert, G. E. (2018). Development and psychometric evaluation of the facilitator competency rubric. *Nursing Education Perspectives, 39*(6), E3–E9. https://doi.org/10.1097/01.NEP.0000000000000409

Lewis, C. C., Fretwell, C. E., Ryan, J., & Parham, J. B. (2013). Faculty use of established and emerging technologies in higher education: A unified theory of acceptance and use of technology perspective. *International Journal of Higher Education, 2*(2), 22–34. https://doi.org/10.5430/ijhe.v2n2p22

Lockee, B. B. (2021). Shifting digital, shifting context: (Re)considering teacher professional development for online and blended learning in the COVID-19 era. *Educational Technology Research and Development, 69*(1), 17–20. https://doi.org/10.1007/s11423-020-09836-8

Lowenthal, P. R., & Hodges, C. B. (2015). In search of quality: Using quality matters to analyze the quality of massive, open, online courses (MOOCs). *International Review of Research in Open and Distributed Learning, 16*(5), 83–101. https://doi.org/10.19173/irrodl.v16i5.2348

Martin, F. (2011). Instructional design process and the importance of instructional alignment. *Community College Journal of Research and Practice, 35*(12), 955–972. https://doi.org/10.1080/10668920802466483

Martin, F., Bolliger, D., & Flowers, C. (2021). Design matters: Development and validation of the online course design elements (OCDE) instrument. *International Review of Research in Open and Distributed Learning, 22*(2), 46–71. https://doi.org/10.19173/irrodl.v22i2.5187

Martin, F., Budhrani, K., Kumar, S., & Ritzhaupt, A. (2019). Award-winning faculty online teaching practices: Roles and competencies. *Online Learning, 23*(1), 184–205. https://doi.org/10.24059/olj.v23i1.1329

Martin, F., Budhrani, K., & Wang, C. (2019). Examining faculty perception of their readiness to teach online. *Online Learning, 23*(3), 97–119. https://doi.org/10.24059/olj.v23i3.1555

Martin, F., Kumar, S., & She, L. (2021). Examining higher education instructor perceptions of roles and competencies in online teaching. *Online Learning, 25*(4), 267–295. https://doi.org/10.24059/olj.v25i4.2570

Martin, F., Wang, C., & Sadaf, A. (2018). Student perception of helpfulness of facilitation strategies that enhance instructor presence, connectedness, engagement and learning in online courses. *The Internet and Higher Education, 37*, 52–65. https://doi.org/10.1016/j.iheduc.2018.01.003

McGroarty, M. (1985). Language proficiency, technical skill, and vocational awareness: Instructor competencies for bilingual vocational training. *NABE Journal, 9*(2), 25–40. https://doi.org/10.1080/08855072.1985.10668490

Mehmet, K. A. R. A., Kukul, V., & Çakir, R. (2018). Conceptions and misconceptions of instructors pertaining to their roles and competencies in distance education: A qualitative case study. *Participatory Educational Research, 5*(2), 67–79. http://doi.org/10.17275/per.18.12.5.2

Moore, K. D. (2014). *Effective instructional strategies: From theory to practice.* SAGE Publications.

Mullet, H. G., Butler, A. C., Verdin, B., von Borries, R., & Marsh, E. J. (2014). Delaying feedback promotes transfer of knowledge despite student preferences to receive feedback immediately. *Journal of Applied Research in Memory and Cognition, 3*(3), 222–229. https://doi.org/10.1016/j.jarmac.2014.05.001

Newmann, F. M., Wehlage, G. G., & Lamborn, S. D. (1992). The significance and sources of student engagement. In F. Newmann (Ed.), *Student engagement and achievement in American secondary schools* (pp. 11–39). Teachers College Press.

Oyarzun, B., Martin, F., & Moore, R. (2020). Time management matters: Online faculty perceptions of helpfulness of time. *Distance Education, 41*(1), 106–127. https://doi.org/10.1080/01587919.2020.1724773

Parr, J. D. (1976). *Essential and desirable music and music-teaching competencies for first-year band instructors in the public schools* [Doctoral dissertation, The University of Iowa]. https://www.proquest.com/openview/2dc5c416ed232149396e017c73889f80

Patton, K. K., Branzetti, J. B., & Robins, L. (2016). Assessment and the competencies: A faculty development game. *Journal of Graduate Medical Education, 8*(3), 442–443. https://doi.org/10.4300/JGME-D-15-00596.1

Phelps, A., & Vlachopoulos, D. (2020). Successful transition to synchronous learning environments in distance education: A research on entry-level synchronous facilitator competencies. *Education and Information Technologies, 25*, 1511–1527. https://doi.org/10.1007/s10639-019-09989-x

Pulham, E., Graham, C., & Short, C. (2018). Generic vs. modality-specific competencies for K–12 online and blended teaching. *Journal of Online Learning Research, 4*(1), 33–52. https://eric.ed.gov/?id=EJ1174455

Ryan, S. J. (1987). *Instructor competencies required for effective fieldwork supervision of occupational therapy and physical therapy students* [Doctoral dissertation, University of British Columbia]. https://open.library.ubc.ca/soa/cIRcle/collections/ubctheses/831/items/1.0097068

Sali-ot, M. A. (2011). Competencies of instructors: Its correlation to the factors affecting the academic performance of students. *JPAIR Multidisciplinary Research Journal, 6*(1). https://ejournals.ph/article.php?id=7468

Saskatchewan Education Department. (1991). *Instructional approaches: A framework for professional practice.* Saskatchewan Education. https://eric.ed.gov/?id=ED 340692

Senemoglu, N., Beyaztas, D. I., & Kapti, S. B. (2016). Graduate students' opinions of professors' competencies in graduate schools of education. *Journal of the International Society for Teacher Education, 20*(2), 79–92. https://files.eric.ed.gov/fulltext/EJ1177045.pdf

Sims, L., & Falkenberg, T. (2013). Developing competencies for education for sustainable development: A case study of Canadian faculties of education. *International Journal of Higher Education, 2*(4), 1–14. http://doi.org/10.5430/ijhe.v2n4p1

Thomas, J. E., & Graham, C. R. (2019). Online teaching competencies in observational rubrics: What are institutions evaluating? *Distance Education, 40*(1), 114–132. https://doi.org/10.1080/01587919.2018.1553564

Tobin, T. J., Mandernach, B. J., & Taylor, A. H. (2015). *Evaluating online teaching: Implementing best practices.* Jossey-Bass.

Uttl, B., White, C. A., & Gonzalez, D. W. (2017). Meta-analysis of faculty's teaching effectiveness: Student evaluation of teaching ratings and student learning are not related. *Studies in Educational Evaluation, 54*, 22–42. https://doi.org/10.1016/j.stueduc.2016.08.007

Valiee, S., Moridi, G., Khaledi, S., & Garibi, F. (2016). Nursing students' perspectives on clinical instructors' effective teaching strategies: A descriptive study. *Nurse Education in Practice, 16*(1), 258–262. https://doi.org/10.1016/j.nepr.2015.09.009

Yıldırım, İ. (2021). A study on the effect of instructors' communication skills on the professional attitudes and self-efficacy of student teachers. *Journal of Education for Teaching, 47*(4), 605–620. https://doi.org/10.1080/02607476.2021.1902237

CHAPTER 4

VALIDATION OF COMPETENCIES

CHAPTER OVERVIEW

This chapter first provides an overview of the validation processes used to create the new 2021 IBSTPI instructor performance statements, competencies, and domains. Next, we discuss the administration of a survey on a cross-sectional sample of instructors from different backgrounds, contexts, and experiences from across the globe. These data are analyzed to provide further validity and reliability evidence of the individual performance statements, competencies, and the domains included in the 2021 IBSTPI instructor competencies. Additionally, the demographic characteristics of the sample of instructors are provided to characterize the results.

Orienting Questions

- What are the research-based validation processes used to create a survey to assess the validity and reliability of the instructor performance statements, competencies, and domains?
- What are the instructor demographic characteristics (gender, age, geographic location, highest degree earned, and teaching

Instructor Competencies, pages 55–68
Copyright © 2023 by Information Age Publishing
www.infoagepub.com
All rights of reproduction in any form reserved.

> experience) of the sample of instructors?
> - What evidence of content and construct validity and reliability can be provided about the 2021 IBSTPI instructor competencies using our sample of instructors?

DEVELOPMENT OF SURVEY

Data Collection Process

The survey was distributed across social media networks, a link on the IBSTPI webpage, and listservs on the Internet known to be used by instructors across national borders. The survey remained open for a period of approximately 6 months, and during this period several reminder posts and emails were issued to collect the broadest possible sample of instructors with core, blended, and online teaching experiences.

Demographic Characteristics of Sample

Table 4.1 provides the demographic characteristics of the sample of $N = 578$ instructors. As can be gleaned, approximately 55% of the sample were female and the others were male, with a few missing responses. The survey did include an "other" option for gender, but this selection was not used by the participants. More than three-quarters of the participants were between the ages of 20 and 59, and more than 60% of the participants held a master's or doctoral degree. More than two-thirds of the participants were within the United States or Canada. Finally, as shown, the participants had a wide range of core, blended, and online teaching experiences.

DATA ANALYSIS

The survey data were analyzed using descriptive statistics, exploratory factor analysis (EFA), internal consistency reliability, multivariate analysis of variance (MANOVA), and analysis of variance (ANOVA) as a follow-up procedure, and finally, Pearson correlation analysis. Additionally, the assumptions (e.g., homogeneity of the variance) of each data analysis approach were examined prior to executing the analyses. Descriptive statistics were used to provide the mean and standard deviations of the data. EFA was employed to demonstrate the multidimensional nature of each of the domains

Validation of Competencies • 57

TABLE 4.1   Demographic Characteristics of the Sample of Instructors

Gender	n	%
Male	255	44.1
Female	316	54.7
Total	571	98.8
Missing Response	7	1.2

Age Range	n	%
20 to 39	118	20.4
40 to 49	155	26.8
50 to 59	186	32.2
60 or above	118	20.4
Total	577	99.8
Missing Response	1	0.2

Education Level	n	%
Doctorate	172	29.8
Master's	208	36.0
Associate/Bachelor's	84	14.5
Other	114	19.7
Total	578	100.0

Geographic Location	n	%
United States (US) or Canada	392	67.8
Outside US or Canada	186	32.2
Total	578	100.0

Core Teaching Experience	n	%
I have not been an instructor in this setting	15	2.6
Less than 5 years	76	13.2
5 to 10 years	116	20.1
More than 10 years	371	64.2
Total	578	100.0

Blended Teaching Experience	n	%
I have not been an instructor in this setting	85	14.7
Less than 5 years	154	26.6
5 to 10 years	147	25.4
More than 10 years	192	33.2
Total	578	100.0

Online Teaching Experience	n	%
I have not been an instructor in this setting	145	25.1
Less than 5 years	169	29.2
5 to 10 years	121	20.9
More than 10 years	143	24.7
Total	578	100.0

as separate EFA models were examined for each domain and its associated performance statements. MANOVA and ANOVA were used to illustrate the differences among the competencies across the demographic variables. Finally, correlation analyses were used to show the relationships among the competencies in each domain.

Please note that the descriptive statistics for each domain, competency, and performance statement are provided in the ensuing chapters. We also provide the MANOVA and ANOVA results within each respective chapter. Within this chapter, we provide the EFA for the professional foundations, designing for learning, facilitating learning, and evaluating learning domains across the core competencies, blended competencies, and online competencies. The EFA models were executed using principal axis factoring and an oblique (promax) rotation, as the competencies were anticipated to be related to represent the larger domains.

Validation Results

The results section first presents the details associated with each domain: (a) Professional Foundations domain, (b) Designing for Learning domain, (c) Facilitating Learning domain, and (d) Evaluating Learning domain. In each section, we provide a summary of the EFA results by providing the number of performance statements in each section, the Bartlett Test of Sphericity, the Kaiser-Meyer-Olkin measure of sampling adequacy, the performance statement-to-participant ratio, and the cumulative variance explained by the number of competencies within each respective domain. Please note that we do not provide the individual factor loadings for each performance statement per domain. Rather, the results of the EFA are provided to confirm that each domain had sufficient common variance from the intercorrelation matrices, the sample of instructors was sufficient for the EFA models, and the competencies within each domain were multidimensional in nature.

After presenting the results for each domain from the EFA models, we present the internal consistency reliability coefficients for each domain by core, blended and online contexts. We computed Cronbach's α for each measure to provide preliminary reliability evidence for the data and measures for each competency. Finally, we provide the Pearson correlation coefficients between the core and blended, and core and online competencies as further evidence of construct validity across the contexts covered by the 2021 IBSTPI instructor competencies. As noted, the descriptive statistics of the performance statements associated within each domain and competency are provided in the ensuing chapters.

Professional Foundations Domain

The Professional Foundations domain consisted of 56 performance statements across six competencies in the core, blended, and online contexts. The responses from the $N = 578$ sample of instructors were entered into EFA models and we also provide the Bartlett's test of sphericity, the Kaiser-Meyer-Olkin measure of sampling adequacy, the performance statement-to-participant ratios for each model, and the cumulative variance explained by the six competencies in the Professional Foundations domain. Table 4.2 summarizes these data for readers and shows the data meet the basic requirements for the models. The competencies within the Professional Foundations domain include:

1. Effective Communication
2. Improvement of Instructor Practices
3. Anticipation of Situational Factors
4. Ethical and Legal Standards
5. Establishment of Professionalism
6. Management of Instructional Resources

Designing for Learning Domain

The Designing for Learning domain consists of 48 performance statements across five competencies in the core, blended, and online contexts. The responses from the $N = 578$ sample of instructors were entered into EFA models, and we also provide the Bartlett's test of sphericity, the Kaiser-Meyer-Olkin measure of sampling adequacy, the performance statement-to-participant ratios for each model, and the cumulative variance explained by the five competencies in the Designing for Learning domain. Table 4.3 summarizes these data for readers and shows the data meet the basic requirements for the models. The five competencies within the Designing for Learning domain include:

TABLE 4.2 Data Summary for the Professional Foundations Domain

Criterion	Core	Blended	Online
Number of Performance Statements in Domain	28	12	16
Bartlett Test of Sphericity	Chi-square of 9,151.49 ($p < .001$)	Chi-square of 3,255.77 ($p < .001$)	Chi-square of 5,114.54 ($p < .001$)
Kaiser-Meyer-Olkin Measure of Sampling Adequacy	0.936	0.875	0.912
Performance Statement-to-Participant Ratio	1:21	1:48	1:36
Cumulative Variance Explained by Number of Competencies	69.34% (6)	87.43% (6)	82.94% (6)

TABLE 4.3 Data Summary for the Designing for Learning Domain

Criterion	Competencies		
	Core	Blended	Online
Number of Performance Statements in Domain	20	14	14
Bartlett Test of Sphericity	Chi-square of 6,650.90 ($p < .001$)	Chi-square of 4,740.98 ($p < .001$)	Chi-square of 5,525.42 ($p < .001$)
Kaiser-Meyer-Olkin Measure of Sampling Adequacy	0.951	0.942	0.937
Performance Statement-to-Participant Ratio	1:29	1:41	1:41
Cumulative Variance Explained by Number of Competencies	77.01% (5)	86.02% (5)	89.06% (5)

7. Specification of Expected Learning
8. Plan Instructional Approach
9. Plan of Instructional Resources
10. Preparation of Instructional/Learning Activities
11. Preparation of Assessment and Feedback

Facilitating Learning Domain

The Facilitating Learning domain consisted of 42 performance statements across six competencies in the core, blended, and online contexts. The responses from the $N = 578$ sample of instructors were entered into EFA models and we also provide the Bartlett's test of sphericity, the Kaiser-Meyer-Olkin measure of sampling adequacy, the performance statement-to-participant ratios for each model, and the cumulative variance explained by the six competencies in the Facilitating Learning domain. Table 4.4 summarizes these data for readers and shows that the data meet the basic requirements for the models. The six competencies within the Facilitating Learning domain include:

12. Learner Engagement
13. Instruction Adaptation To Learners/Learning Environment
14. Learning Promotion Through Feedback
15. Retention and Promotion of Knowledge, Skills, and Attitudes
16. Transfer of Learned Knowledge, Skills, and Attitudes to Other Contexts
17. Application of Class Management Principles

Evaluating Learning Domain

The Evaluating Learning domain consisted of 17 performance statements across two competencies in the core, blended, and online contexts. The responses from the $N = 578$ sample of instructors were entered into EFA models

TABLE 4.4 Data Summary for the Facilitating Learning Domain

Criterion	Competencies		
	Core	Blended	Online
Number of Performance Statements in Domain	21	11	10
Bartlett Test of Sphericity	Chi-square of 6,053.99 ($p < .001$)	Chi-square of 2,943.62 ($p < .001$)	Chi-square of 3,327.84 ($p < .001$)
Kaiser-Meyer-Olkin Measure of Sampling Adequacy	0.918	0.900	0.918
Performance Statement-to-Participant Ratio	1:28	1:53	1:58
Cumulative Variance Explained by Number of Competencies	71.94% (6)	87.62% (6)	92.49% (6)

and we also provide the Bartlett's test of sphericity, the Kaiser-Meyer-Olkin measure of sampling adequacy, the performance statement to participant ratios for each model, and the cumulative variance explained by the two competencies in the Evaluating Learning domain. Table 4.5 summarizes these data for readers and shows the data meet the basic requirements for the models. The two competencies within the Evaluating Learning domain include:

18. Plan and Preparation for Monitoring and Evaluating Instruction
19. Evaluation of Instructional Effectiveness

Internal Consistency Reliability

Each competency by core, blended, and online context was analyzed for internal consistency reliability using the Cronbach's α coefficient. Notably, the Cronbach's α coefficient for a measure is deemed acceptable if the value is greater than $\alpha = 0.70$. As can be gleaned in Table 4.6, all of the

TABLE 4.5 Data Summary for the Evaluating Learning Domain

Criterion	Competencies		
	Core	Blended	Online
Number of Performance Statements in Domain	10	4	3
Bartlett Test of Sphericity	Chi-square of 4,379.77 ($p < .001$)	Chi-square of 1,390.31 ($p < .001$)	Chi-square of 491.30 ($p < .001$)
Kaiser-Meyer-Olkin Measure of Sampling Adequacy	0.924	0.846	0.708
Performance Statement-to-Participant Ratio	1:58	1:145	1:193
Cumulative Variance Explained by Number of Competencies	78.71% (2)	91.74% (2)	90.14% (2)

TABLE 4.6 Internal Consistency Reliability of the Data

Competency Contexts	Competencies					
	Core		Blended		Online	
Domain/Competency	α	# of items	α	# of items	α	# of items
Professional Foundations						
1. Effective Communication	0.854	5	0.835	3	0.896	5
2. Improvement of Instructor Practices	0.853	5	0.802	2	0.870	2
3. Anticipation of Situational Factors	0.905	4	0.902	3	0.835	2
4. Ethical and Legal Standards	0.915	5	0.904	2	0.920	2
5. Establishment of Professionalism	0.850	6	0.850	3	0.902	3
6. Management of Instructional Resources	0.800	3	0.905	2	0.838	2
Designing for Learning						
7. Specification of Expected Learning	0.878	4	0.838	3	0.921	2
8. Plan Instructional Approach	0.876	3	0.851	2	0.824	2
9. Plan of Instructional Resources	0.889	4	0.857	2	0.903	2
10. Preparation of Instructional/Learning Activities	0.862	5	0.871	2	0.903	3
11. Preparation of Assessment and Feedback	0.890	4	0.932	5	0.943	5
Facilitating Learning						
12. Learner Engagement	0.784	3	0.863	3	0.914	2
13. Instruction Adaptation to Learners/Learning Environment	0.832	3	—	1	0.890	2
14. Learning Promotion Through Feedback	0.801	3	0.867	3	0.919	3
15. Retention and Promotion of Knowledge, Skills, and Attitudes	0.852	5	—	1	—	1
16. Transfer of Learned Knowledge, Skills, and Attitudes to Other Contexts	0.804	3	—	1	—	1
17. Application of Class Management Principles	0.867	4	0.874	2	—	1
Evaluating Learning						
18. Plan and Preparation for Monitoring and Evaluating Instruction	0.937	5	0.938	3	0.822	2
19. Evaluation of Instructional Effectiveness	0.923	5	—	1	—	1

Cronbach's α coefficients are above this social science threshold, and thus, our data appear to be internally consistent for each competency within each respective domain. Please note that a few competencies only contained a single performance statement, and thus, a Cronbach's α coefficient could not be provided.

Correlations Across Contexts

Correlations Between Core and Blended Context

Table 4.7 and Table 4.8 provide the Pearson correlation coefficients between the core and blended context competencies in the 2021 IBSTPI instructor competencies. Correlation coefficients tell us two things about the nature of the relationship between two variables: (a) the strength of the relationship and (b) the direction of the relationship (positive, no relationship, negative). With this in mind, as shown in both tables, all of the correlation coefficients are positive and significant at a .01 level, which provides further evidence of construct validity of the 21 IBSTPI instructor competencies. These relationships are expected to be both related and positive in nature since none of the competencies are stated negatively.

Correlation Between Core and Online Contexts

Table 4.9 and Table 4.10 provide the Pearson correlation coefficients between the core and online context competencies in the 2021 IBSTPI instructor competencies. Correlation coefficients tell us two things about the nature of the relationship between two variables: (a) the strength of the relationship and (b) the direction of the relationship (positive, no relationship, negative). As shown in both tables, all the correlation coefficients are positive and significant at a .01 level, which provides further evidence of construct validity of the 21 IBSTPI instructor competencies. These relationships are expected to be both related and positive in nature since none of the competencies are stated negatively.

CONCLUSION

This chapter provides the processes used to provide stronger evidence of validity and reliability of the 2021 IBSTPI instructor competencies. We created a survey aligned to the 2021 IBSTPI instructor competencies following systematic procedures and best practices in survey development. Subsequently, we administered this survey to $N = 578$ instructors from across the globe to provide further evidence of the validity and reliability of the 2021 IBSTPI instructor competencies across the core, blended, and online contexts.

64 ▪ Instructor Competencies

TABLE 4.7 Pearson Correlation Coefficients Between Core and Blended Competencies

Competencies	1	2	3	4	5	6	7	8	9	10
					Blended					
Core 1	.611**	.398**	.343**	.447**	.513**	.424**	.314**	.325**	.377**	.329**
Core 2	.438**	.658**	.523**	.434**	.506**	.536**	.387**	.389**	.467**	.429**
Core 3	.386**	.514**	.717**	.399**	.493**	.565**	.452**	.476**	.535**	.500**
Core 4	.343**	.382**	.418**	.850**	.425**	.427**	.319**	.333**	.331**	.373**
Core 5	.459**	.495**	.428**	.431**	.784**	.548**	.378**	.368**	.432**	.365**
Core 6	.429**	.503**	.508**	.509**	.530**	.756**	.439**	.435**	.524**	.473**
Core 7	.331**	.338**	.434**	.261**	.402**	.416**	.669**	.489**	.519**	.465**
Core 8	.370**	.370**	.508**	.269**	.443**	.452**	.666**	.636**	.604**	.559**
Core 9	.412**	.448**	.507**	.390**	.474**	.525**	.585**	.579**	.776**	.610**
Core 10	.380**	.421**	.494**	.376**	.514**	.477**	.550**	.548**	.667**	.685**
Core 11	.396**	.419**	.521**	.299**	.462**	.519**	.594**	.586**	.615**	.571**
Core 12	.386**	.369**	.373**	.304**	.472**	.429**	.366**	.383**	.411**	.397**
Core 13	.385**	.414**	.438**	.305**	.432**	.428**	.376**	.372**	.432**	.401**
Core 14	.327**	.337**	.319**	.336**	.405**	.379**	.335**	.328**	.346**	.355**
Core 15	.393**	.412**	.409**	.337**	.440**	.387**	.398**	.349**	.436**	.425**
Core 16	.369**	.400**	.368**	.377**	.411**	.422**	.388**	.360**	.402**	.340**
Core 17	.381**	.358**	.398**	.441**	.440**	.456**	.343**	.313**	.397**	.353**
Core 18	.268**	.367**	.448**	.337**	.409**	.489**	.548**	.484**	.454**	.439**
Core 19	.251**	.341**	.421**	.211**	.406**	.490**	.447**	.375**	.465**	.396**

* $p < .05$; ** $p < .01$

TABLE 4.8 Pearson Correlation Coefficients Between Core and Blended Competencies (Continued)

Competencies	11	12	13	14	15	16	17	18	19
Core 1	.330**	.391**	.299**	.361**	.338**	.307**	.420**	.260**	.214**
Core 2	.432**	.399**	.346**	.475**	.430**	.416**	.504**	.335**	.343**
Core 3	.529**	.449**	.413**	.471**	.436**	.429**	.488**	.469**	.415**
Core 4	.321**	.254**	.260**	.263**	.251**	.266**	.402**	.316**	.240**
Core 5	.432**	.515**	.349**	.434**	.370**	.374**	.458**	.352**	.281**
Core 6	.506**	.413**	.379**	.474**	.399**	.394**	.568**	.493**	.369**
Core 7	.532**	.418**	.312**	.392**	.377**	.353**	.383**	.485**	.349**
Core 8	.584**	.412**	.363**	.389**	.402**	.364**	.378**	.469**	.334**
Core 9	.566**	.423**	.420**	.452**	.465**	.408**	.471**	.486**	.412**
Core 10	.547**	.459**	.427**	.457**	.460**	.415**	.456**	.444**	.375**
Core 11	.795**	.506**	.480**	.563**	.455**	.413**	.457**	.572**	.467**
Core 12	.407**	.580**	.399**	.449**	.361**	.361**	.400**	.302**	.268**
Core 13	.443**	.483**	.704**	.525**	.430**	.411**	.509**	.397**	.353**
Core 14	.419**	.392**	.378**	.604**	.388**	.413**	.408**	.371**	.298**
Core 15	.432**	.448**	.431**	.537**	.624**	.507**	.496**	.353**	.321**
Core 16	.424**	.394**	.324**	.463**	.444**	.672**	.441**	.385**	.336**
Core 17	.342**	.355**	.362**	.399**	.382**	.343**	.668**	.351**	.299**
Core 18	.542**	.373**	.359**	.389**	.271**	.365**	.381**	.730**	.551**
Core 19	.530**	.378**	.415**	.466**	.340**	.379**	.358**	.591**	.747**

* $p < .05$; ** $p < .01$

66 ▪ Instructor Competencies

TABLE 4.9 Pearson Correlation Coefficients Between Core and Online Competencies

Competencies	1	2	3	4	5	6	7	8	9	10
Core 1	.646**	.340**	.349**	.435**	.475**	.421**	.272**	.353**	.340**	.340**
Core 2	.466**	.597**	.455**	.411**	.475**	.513**	.311**	.437**	.418**	.482**
Core 3	.442**	.465**	.668**	.402**	.463**	.557**	.439**	.526**	.504**	.537**
Core 4	.455**	.339**	.441**	.796**	.356**	.375**	.313**	.341**	.327**	.353**
Core 5	.512**	.439**	.420**	.408**	.710**	.538**	.350**	.460**	.396**	.417**
Core 6	.458**	.467**	.504**	.436**	.455**	.699**	.317**	.425**	.452**	.468**
Core 7	.374**	.321**	.435**	.302**	.407**	.375**	.603**	.524**	.462**	.464**
Core 8	.365**	.363**	.496**	.276**	.438**	.423**	.551**	.646**	.537**	.532**
Core 9	.506**	.414**	.538**	.393**	.474**	.542**	.563**	.588**	.697**	.626**
Core 10	.469**	.425**	.537**	.423**	.506**	.508**	.488**	.591**	.605**	.691**
Core 11	.463**	.411**	.517**	.330**	.492**	.527**	.519**	.600**	.569**	.579**
Core 12	.442**	.346**	.380**	.312**	.449**	.443**	.315**	.375**	.409**	.433**
Core 13	.382**	.346**	.407**	.289**	.437**	.394**	.367**	.427**	.348**	.411**
Core 14	.451**	.327**	.355**	.379**	.419**	.368**	.380**	.396**	.331**	.398**
Core 15	.438**	.347**	.428**	.340**	.423**	.413**	.398**	.428**	.408**	.467**
Core 16	.422**	.316**	.390**	.429**	.440**	.392**	.316**	.388**	.386**	.407**
Core 17	.394**	.345**	.382**	.410**	.363**	.407**	.273**	.337**	.298**	.380**
Core 18	.269**	.266**	.428**	.303**	.348**	.425**	.444**	.445**	.442**	.396**
Core 19	.276**	.270**	.383**	.212**	.366**	.423**	.388**	.434**	.414**	.376**

Online

* $p < .05$; ** $p < .01$

Validation of Competencies • 67

TABLE 4.10 Pearson Correlation Coefficients Between Core and Online Competencies (Continued)

Competencies	11	12	13	14	Online 15	16	17	18	19
Core 1	.356**	.338**	.309**	.329**	.292**	.289**	.347**	.277**	.232**
Core 2	.421**	.386**	.413**	.447**	.400**	.380**	.472**	.331**	.350**
Core 3	.529**	.438**	.442**	.452**	.415**	.440**	.420**	.445**	.397**
Core 4	.342**	.303**	.349**	.332**	.271**	.297**	.354**	.307**	.242**
Core 5	.500**	.442**	.385**	.428**	.430**	.377**	.414**	.435**	.317**
Core 6	.541**	.337**	.401**	.401**	.380**	.338**	.438**	.522**	.360**
Core 7	.514**	.410**	.324**	.391**	.308**	.325**	.323**	.426**	.320**
Core 8	.567**	.393**	.391**	.418**	.391**	.385**	.362**	.410**	.355**
Core 9	.582**	.463**	.481**	.444**	.427**	.429**	.426**	.444**	.439**
Core 10	.588**	.487**	.496**	.502**	.474**	.419**	.439**	.472**	.452**
Core 11	.726**	.497**	.556**	.576**	.489**	.439**	.443**	.515**	.442**
Core 12	.422**	.527**	.432**	.481**	.401**	.358**	.380**	.318**	.291**
Core 13	.447**	.392**	.643**	.496**	.407**	.381**	.391**	.369**	.314**
Core 14	.458**	.364**	.417**	.546**	.368**	.393**	.369**	.344**	.302**
Core 15	.438**	.395**	.454**	.466**	.573**	.469**	.428**	.321**	.332**
Core 16	.418**	.340**	.352**	.415**	.418**	.562**	.365**	.356**	.372**
Core 17	.350**	.290**	.375**	.351**	.306**	.247**	.518**	.321**	.281**
Core 18	.516**	.352**	.338**	.400**	.259**	.342**	.322**	.685**	.517**
Core 19	.522**	.399**	.392**	.391**	.260**	.330**	.310**	.564**	.738**

* $p < .05$; ** $p < .01$

Our results demonstrate that the domains of Professional Foundations, Designing for Learning, Facilitating Learning, and Evaluating Learning are multidimensional in nature. While the individual performance statements and larger constructs as our competencies may not capture all aspects of the role of an instructor across the core, blended, and online contexts, we believe we have provided strong preliminary evidence to demonstrate the 2021 IBSTPI instructor competencies are both relevant and important to the evolving role of instructors irrespective of settings (e.g., higher education, military, or corporate) and instructional technologies (e.g., specific learning management systems like Canvas or Blackboard). The following chapters break down the individual performance statements, competencies, and domains that constitute the 2021 IBSTPI instructor competencies across the core, blended, and online contexts.

CHAPTER 5

CORE INSTRUCTOR COMPETENCIES

> **CHAPTER OVERVIEW**
>
> This chapter focuses broadly on the competencies of instructors across all types of instructional settings (e.g., face-to-face, blended, or online) with or without the use of technology. IBSTPI's core instructor competencies, conceived as essential competencies for instructors irrespective of different types of instructional configurations, are based on empirical findings and expert review. We provide a detailed account of the four domains, 19 competencies, and associated core performance statements with the descriptive statistics from the validation as supporting evidence.
>
> **Orienting Questions**
>
> - What competencies and performances do instructors consider critical to teaching, irrespective of context, learner types, and subject matter?
> - What instructor demographic characteristics (gender, age, geographic location, highest degree earned, online teaching experience) are related to core competencies for instructors?

CORE INSTRUCTOR COMPETENCIES

Competent instructors are instrumental in creating effective teaching and learning. The core instructor competencies, identified following the IBSTPI competency development model described in Chapter 2, are organized into four domains and 19 competencies and have 79 supporting performance statements. The four larger domains of competencies include: (a) Foundations, (b) Designing for Learning, (c) Facilitating Learning, and (d) Evaluation of Learning. In the subsequent sections, we describe the four domains and 19 competencies using the validation results of the individual performance statements. The instructors were asked to rate the competencies on a five-point Likert scale: *not critical* = 1, *slightly critical* = 2, *moderately critical* = 3, *critical* = 4, *highly critical* = 5.

Participants

Table 5.1 provides the demographic characteristics of the participants who completed the core competencies section of the validation survey.

Foundations

The domain of Foundations competencies is intended to operationalize the many dimensions of instructors across delivery methods, contexts, and types of learners. While certain competencies are often described as hallmarks of effective instructional and learning experiences as guided by an instructor (e.g., effective communication), other competencies are professional expectations necessary for the craft of effective teaching.

1. Effective Communication

Instructors are communicators of complex ideas from their subject domains and are tasked with providing their learners with feedback and guidance to ensure learning outcomes are achieved. Thus, the act of communication is a foundation for all instructors. Instructors must choose the appropriate medium, compose an intentional message, and systematically engage their learners in one-on-one, group, and whole group communication in a respectful and culturally sensitive manner. It is imperative that instructors use concise, consistent, and clear vocabulary appropriate to the learner and the purpose of the communication. Communication skills go beyond what is written and spoken, for individuals communicate nonverbally using body language and listening skills; thus, an instructor needs to be well-versed in all aspects of communicating. Instructors will need to identify and

TABLE 5.1 Demographic Characteristics of the Core Competencies Survey Participants

Demographic Variables	n	%
Gender		
Male	189	47.13%
Female	212	52.87%
Age Range		
20 to 39	76	18.77%
40 to 49	105	25.93%
50 to 59	139	34.32%
60 and over	85	20.99%
Geographic Location		
United States or Canada	288	70.94%
Outside the United States or Canada	118	29.06%
Educational Level		
Doctorate	122	30.05%
Master's Degree	144	35.47%
Undergraduate 2- or 4-year	61	15.02%
Other	79	19.46%
Face-to-Face Teaching Experience		
Less than 5 years	54	13.67%
5 to 10 years	72	18.23%
More than 10 years	269	68.10%

select the means of communicating based on what is best for the different types of communication and seek out differences in cultural uses of language including, for example, the use of gestures and eye contact. By taking into consideration the reciprocal influence of various factors, such as context, tools, and purpose, an instructor will be able to provide an optimal means of communication. As supported by the validation results, effective communication is a Foundation competency identified as critical as shown in Table 5.2.

2. Improvement of Instructor Practices

Instructors should be open-minded to the various sources of feedback and activities for their own professional growth, in an effort to promote improved instructional practices. As shown in Table 5.3, instructors can improve their instructional practices by engaging in deliberate activities to seek guidance from others, engage in reflective activities, and seek peer professional development opportunities. Fundamental to ongoing improvement is an instructor's ability to actively seek and listen to other stakeholders' perspectives that

TABLE 5.2 Competencies Related to Effective Communication

Competency performance statements	N	M	SD
1.a Express oneself clearly	578	4.70	0.62
1.b Ensure consistency and coherence of messages across all communications	577	4.57	0.69
1.c Communicate systematically	575	4.38	0.76
1.d Use respectful language	574	4.63	0.68
1.e Communicate with sensitivity to cultural differences	578	4.49	0.77

TABLE 5.3 Competencies Related to Improvement of Instructor Practices

Competency performance statements	N	M	SD
2.a Balance working alone and in collaboration	564	3.84	0.98
2.b Seek and share input from multiple and diverse perspectives	564	4.11	0.85
2.c Engage in self-reflective activities to improve practice	564	4.31	0.83
2.d Demonstrate openness to change and improvement	564	4.46	0.74
2.e Support peer professional development	562	4.18	0.90

can validate personal perspectives and also provide different perspectives. When instructors self-reflect on what they learn from others and on their own thoughts, practices, and evidence, they will develop new insights about themselves and how best to reach their learners. Ultimately, a mindset of openness to change and continuous improvement are necessary.

3. Anticipation of Situational Factors

Instructors must be capable of anticipating a range of situational variables from the instructional environment and the participants involved in such programs, including characteristics of the stakeholders, the instructional context, the subject matter domain, and an overall assessment of the target learners. An instructor may need to assess a number of factors including, for example, learners' visual literacy or technology readiness. These performance statements are illustrated in Table 5.4 and form a foundational competency akin to instructional design models that encourage careful analysis of the context, learners, and context to arrange effective and efficient instructional programs (Dick et al., 2005).

4. Ethical and Legal Standards

Instructors and other stakeholders involved in instructional programs are a part of a larger ecosystem of regulatory and ethical considerations.

TABLE 5.4 Competencies Related to Anticipation of Situational Factors

Competency performance statements	N	M	SD
3.a Determine relevant characteristics of stakeholders	548	3.97	0.94
3.b Determine characteristics of context	550	4.02	0.88
3.c Determine characteristics of content	548	4.06	0.90
3.d Determine level of learners' familiarity with resources, technologies, procedures, and processes	552	4.11	0.91

TABLE 5.5 Competencies Related to Ethical and Legal Standards

Competency performance statements	N	M	SD
4.a Recognize ethical and legal implications of instructional practices	545	4.51	0.78
4.b Comply with organizational and professional codes of ethics	546	4.63	0.72
4.c Avoid conflicts of interest	545	4.43	0.85
4.d Ensure respect of intellectual property rights	546	4.56	0.74
4.e Avoid situations that would violate privacy rights	544	4.60	0.70

Thus, instructors should be knowledgeable of the relevant considerations impacting their instructional practice and in their setting. Table 5.5 illustrates the performance statements surrounding the regulatory and ethical dimensions, such as conflicts of interest, intellectual property rights, and professional codes of ethics.

5. Establishment of Professionalism

Instructors are professionals and should exhibit professional behaviors and attitudes consistent with their professional settings. By modeling exemplary behavior and attitudes, an instructor comes across as credible and trustworthy. In addition to demonstrating clear expertise in the subject matter in which they instruct, instructors should also have a deep understanding of learning, instruction, and assessment principles. Further, instructors should seek to apply the best practices in their settings while keeping abreast of emerging technologies for instructional applications. These performance statements are shown in Table 5.6.

6. Management of Instructional Resources

With the increasing diversity of instructional environments and domains (e.g., online or blended) for delivery, instructors must become adept in managing the wide range of instructional resources, records, and other administrative documents associated with their professional settings.

TABLE 5.6 Competencies Related to Establishment of Professionalism

Competency performance statements	N	M	SD
5.a Model exemplary professional behavior and attitudes	528	4.55	0.71
5.b Expand one's knowledge of learning principles, instruction, assessment, and management strategies	529	4.53	0.70
5.c Demonstrate expertise in subject matter	529	4.42	0.79
5.d Keep current with emerging technologies and their pedagogical uses	528	4.26	0.86
5.e Seek out and apply instructional best practices	528	4.43	0.76
5.f Document one's work as a foundation for future efforts	529	3.92	1.03

TABLE 5.7 Competencies Related to Management of Instructional Resources

Competency performance statements	N	M	SD
6.a Manage instructional resources	524	3.99	0.89
6.b Complete and organize administrative documents	524	3.72	1.04
6.c Maintain security and privacy of organization, learner, and client records	525	4.35	0.89

Instructors are expected to be able to organize, store, access, transmit, and protect instructional resources and documents. Instructor tasks may include, for example, updating materials for reuse or ensuring that materials are inclusive and accessible. These performance statements are deemed core and foundational to the craft of an instructor, as shown in Table 5.7.

Designing for Learning

The domain of Designing for Learning covers a wide range of competencies that address an instructor's capacity to carefully plan learning experiences aligned to the instructional goals and objectives in a given context (e.g., online). The domain of Designing for Learning highlights competencies that generally occur prior to the learning experience and that involve instructors in planning, creating, selecting, and evaluating instructional resources and learning experiences intended to effectively and efficiently meet the learners' needs. That is, instructors must make many decisions about the learners, context, objectives, instructional strategies, and assessment while addressing creative ways to evaluate the goals of the intervention.

7. Specification of Expected Learning

Careful planning and a focus on crafting instruction with the end in mind are keys to the practice of effective instructors, as shown by the

TABLE 5.8 Competencies Related to Specification of Expected Learning

Competency performance statements	N	M	SD
7.a Articulate instructional goals and learning outcomes (objectives)	518	4.57	0.69
7.b Sequence instructional goals and learning outcomes (objectives)	517	4.35	0.84
7.c Ensure alignment between content, instructional goals, learning outcomes (objectives), and assessments	517	4.60	0.71
7.d Ensure alignment of instructional goals across units of instruction	513	4.39	0.83

performance statements in Table 5.8. This planning involves instructors in making decisions about the goals, sequence, and alignment of the learning experiences. An instructor starts with the "big picture" by identifying the instructional goal, a basic statement of intent that is meant to explain "why we do what we do." Instructors must then ensure clear alignment among the objectives, subject matter, and assessments used for learners to demonstrate their learning.

8. Plan Instructional Approach

Instructors using different approaches to instruction—based on their views of principles, beliefs, or ideas about the nature of learning—must choose an overall approach and strategies to create effective learning experiences for their intended audience, as shown in the performance statements in Table 5.9. While no one approach is suitable for every learning situation, instructors are expected to draw upon a wide range of strategies (e.g., active, collaborative, case-based, on-the-job, and problem-centered) for given contexts and learners. This means that instructors must stay abreast of effective instructional, motivational, and learning strategies that are appropriate for a given learner, context, and instructional goal. Instrumental to instructional planning is an integrated assessment approach that focuses on learner progress and utilizes various types of measures (e.g., performance, knowledge, attitudes, and reflections). Assessment measures present opportunities and

TABLE 5.9 Competencies Related to Planning of Instructional Approach

Competency performance statements	N	M	SD
8.a Identify possible learning strategies given the objectives	514	4.30	0.86
8.b Select a variety of appropriate motivational, instructional, and learning strategies	514	4.38	0.83
8.c Integrate assessments with strategies	512	4.32	0.86

challenges that an instructor must identify and address. The types of issues to consider, for example, include scheduling assessment activities, planning feedback mechanisms and strategies, and ensuring integrity of the assessment process and data.

9. Plan of Instructional Resources

As instructors focus on planning a learning experience to address their unique situation, they must both select and create instructional or learning resources that best convey the subject matter. These resources also need to include assessment resources and a possible array of technologies (e.g., laptop, camera, and digital tools). Table 5.10 provides performance statements that emphasize the common behaviors exhibited by instructors as they strive to create optimal learning experiences.

10. Preparation of Instructional/Learning Activities

Effective instructors must anticipate the many facets of their learners, the learning environment, and any instructional resources for the intended learning outcomes. Instructors are the ones to develop or locate existing materials and resources and to make sure they are readily available for the context. Learners' accessibility needs must be taken into account, and while instructors may be the ones who create accessible resources, they may also need to request assistance to ensure compliance. Instructors will need to prepare instructions on how to use and/or access instructional resources, describe learning activities deliverables, create remediation resources, and do other tasks as needed. Table 5.11 shows that the instructors must ensure that the appropriate learning environment is ready for the planned learning experiences, which includes the use of tools, instructional resources, and other tangible and intangible aspects of the learning environment.

TABLE 5.10 Competencies Related to Planning of Instructional Resources

Competency performance statements	N	M	SD
9.a Identify key points, relevant examples, anecdotes, and additional resources	511	4.23	0.85
9.b Develop a plan to create, use, or modify instructional resources	512	4.08	0.94
9.c Ensure integrity of all selected resources	511	4.24	0.92
9.d Select resources to support instruction, learning, and assessment	510	4.21	0.88

TABLE 5.11 Competencies Related to Preparation of Instructional/Learning Activities

Competency performance statements	N	M	SD
10.a Prepare, acquire, and make instructional resources available	512	4.40	0.77
10.b Create instructional resources that are accessible to all learners	511	4.34	0.92
10.c Prepare for possible learner difficulties, common misconceptions, and questions	508	4.33	0.84
10.d Confirm logistics, physical arrangements, readiness of equipment, technology, and tools	510	4.09	0.93
10.e Prepare instructions to help learners attain readiness to complete activities	510	4.25	0.85

11. Preparation of Assessment and Feedback

Effective learning experiences carefully align the instructional objectives, instruction, and assessment activities to ensure effective and efficient learning. Instructors know that assessing the learning requires a great deal of knowledge and skill, as shown by the performance statements in Table 5.12. Depending on the situation, instructors must creatively design and deploy different types of assessments for learners to demonstrate their progress and attainment of learning and performance. Instructors will need to consider strategies for in-person and virtual assessments using a variety of platforms and tools. An instructor should prepare all assessment and measurement means needed to accommodate all learners by taking into account their characteristics and situations. Further, connecting this assessment to meaningful feedback messages to the learners requires instructors to both identify and assess areas for learners to grow.

TABLE 5.12 Competencies Related to Preparation of Assessment and Feedback

Competency performance statements	N	M	SD
11.a Prepare multiple measures and modalities for assessing learner understanding and performance	501	4.18	0.98
11.b Prepare multiple measures and modalities for assessing learner attitudes and reactions	502	3.84	1.09
11.c Prepare instructions to help learners attain readiness to complete assessments	501	4.06	0.98
11.d Prepare for multiple ways to provide feedback	498	3.98	1.07

Facilitating Learning

While the domain of Designing for Learning speaks to the instructor's efforts before the learning experience, the domain of facilitating learning is about those competencies relating to instructors during the learning experience. An instructor is deemed one who co-constructs knowledge during instructional facilitation.

12. Learner Engagement

Table 5.13 shows the performance statements associated with stimulating, sustaining, and closing down learner engagement during a learning experience. We learn when we pay attention; thus, instructors are tasked with gaining and maintaining learner attention, encouraging participation, and fostering meaningful learning experiences. While there are many different definitions and models of learner engagement (Halverson & Graham, 2019), a recurring finding is that instructors who are tactful in engaging their learners are deemed effective instructors (Rajabalee & Santally, 2021). Instructors should aim to engage learners in setting realistic expectations and to nurture self-efficacy perspectives in learners. Throughout instructional facilitation, instructors are to use a variety of strategies and effective questioning techniques and to bring closure to instruction so that learners are able retain and transfer learning.

13. Instruction Adaptation to Learners/Learning Environment

Learning experiences can be influenced by the dynamics of the group of learners and their prior experiences and personalities. Some modifications and adjustments for language learners or visually impaired learners, for example, may be needed. Instructors must be capable of responding to the unique dynamics of the individuals and group and modify the learning experience accordingly, as shown by the performance statements in Table 5.14.

14. Learning Promotion Through Feedback

Feedback remains one of the most efficacious instructional elements in an instructor's arsenal (Hattie, 2012). Thus, instructors must provide learners with clear, timely, specific, and relevant feedback as needed during a learning experience. Central to effective feedback is that an instructor

TABLE 5.13 Competencies Related to Learner Engagement

Competency performance statements	N	M	SD
12.a Stimulate learner engagement and motivation	522	4.63	0.61
12.b Sustain learner engagement and motivation	524	4.58	0.64
12.c Assist learners in bringing learning activities to closure	524	4.27	0.82

TABLE 5.14 Competencies Related to Instruction Adaptation

Competency performance statements	N	M	SD
13.a Respond to group dynamics	522	4.30	0.82
13.b Adjust instruction based on individual and group learning and performance	523	4.32	0.87
13.c Modify learning environment, as needed	520	4.21	0.90

provides and responds to open and fair feedback using a variety of feedback strategies. Equally important, the learners should also be instructed on feedback approaches and mechanisms and afforded opportunities to both give and receive feedback. These performance statements are shown in Table 5.15.

15. Retention and Promotion of Knowledge, Skills, and Attitudes

An instructor's primary goal is to encourage the retention and promotion of their learners' knowledge, skills, and attitudes (KSAs) aligned to the goals of a learning experience. Thus, instructors must both encourage and promote the development of KSAs as shown by the performance statements in Table 5.16. Instructors should encourage their learners through a variety of media to express their thinking and attitudes at appropriate times, and ultimately promote synthesis and integration of the learning experience by promoting practice and self-assessment.

TABLE 5.15 Competencies Related to Learning Promotion Through Feedback

Competency performance statements	N	M	SD
14.a Provide opportunities for learners to request and give feedback	520	4.54	0.69
14.b Provide clear, timely, specific, and relevant feedback	521	4.61	0.68
14.c Instruct learners on feedback mechanisms	519	4.11	0.89

TABLE 5.16 Competencies Related to Retention and Promotion of KSAs

Competency performance statements	N	M	SD
15.a Encourage learners to express their thinking	513	4.47	0.73
15.b Encourage learners to express their attitudes	513	4.06	0.95
15.c Promote synthesis and integration of learning	512	4.52	0.71
15.d Prompt practice	511	4.46	0.73
15.e Stimulate monitoring and self-assessment	511	4.29	0.83

16. Transfer of Learned Knowledge, Skills, and Attitudes to Other Contexts

Ultimately, the outcome of many instructional interventions is the transfer of KSAs learned in one context and applied in a new one. This type of learning outcome is often referred to as transfer of learning (Mayer, 2002). Transfer of learning is difficult to achieve and requires instructors to create learning experiences that enable the learners to apply their learning across multiple contexts, as shown in the performance statements in Table 5.17.

17. Application of Class Management Principles

The term *class management* sounds as if it is restricted to a physical setting, but it is meant to imply an instructional setting, be it physical or virtual. An instructor is responsible for establishing and managing an effective instructional environment that fosters not only learning, but learner well-being. Using a variety of skills and techniques, an instructor needs to create a positive environment for learning by, for example, managing instructional flow and guiding student behaviors, as shown in Table 5.18.

Evaluating Learning

18. Plan and Preparation for Monitoring and Evaluating Instruction

The process of evaluating instruction, intended to provide both formative (i.e., ongoing feedback for improvement) and summative

TABLE 5.17 Competencies Related to Transfer

Competency performance statements	N	M	SD
16.a Use examples and activities representing multiple contexts	509	4.42	0.77
16.b Create opportunities for learners to apply learning in realistic settings	508	4.58	0.73
16.c Prompt learner exploration of the scope and limits of using learning in other contexts	509	4.18	0.89

TABLE 5.18 Competencies Related to Application of Class Management Principles

Competency performance statements	N	M	SD
17.a Establish ground rules and expectations	507	4.28	0.90
17.b Employ time management during instruction	508	4.24	0.90
17.c Maintain a positive learning atmosphere	508	4.57	0.72
17.d Resolve conflicts and problem efficiently, positively, and fairly	505	4.37	0.85

(i.e., evaluate effectiveness) results, is foundational to effective instructional practices. Instructors are often tasked with evaluating instruction to improve instructional tools, methods, and so on, so that learners can achieve their potential; instructional evaluation, however, is also undertaken by stakeholders who have a vested interest in monitoring and enhancing instruction in various contexts. Evaluation activities can be numerous and include, for example, defining the purpose; asking clear and measurable questions; determining method, instruments, and protocols; and conducting analysis. Although an instructor may conduct evaluations of their own instruction, larger-scale evaluation activities generally involve evaluation specialists. Performance statements related to monitoring and evaluation of instruction are shown in Table 5.19.

19. Evaluation of Instructional Effectiveness

Instructional evaluation requires preparation and planning as well as executing the plan, as shown in Table 5.20. A systematic, organized evaluation plan is needed to ensure that the many facets of evaluation are conducted properly and in a timely way. Clear communication is a key to informing learners and other stakeholders about how to access and respond to evaluation instruments. Prompting responses may be necessary once data

TABLE 5.19 Competencies Related to Monitoring and Evaluating Instruction

Competency performance statements	N	M	SD
18.a Identify the purpose, key questions, and options for evaluation	514	4.26	0.90
18.b Determine the method of evaluation	514	4.10	0.98
18.c Prepare evaluation instruments and procedures	513	4.15	0.93
18.d Ensure integrity of evaluation resources and setting	515	4.22	0.96
18.e Prepare directions for evaluation activities	513	4.07	0.98

TABLE 5.20 Competencies Related to Evaluation of Instructional Effectiveness

Competency performance statements	N	M	SD
19.a Implement a systemic evaluation plan	511	4.18	0.96
19.b Manage evaluation data collection	510	4.01	1.02
19.c Examine findings of instructor performance	507	4.18	0.97
19.d Interpret evaluation findings on effectiveness of the instruction	511	4.28	0.88
19.e Issue and implement recommendations for improvement based on findings	512	4.30	0.89

collection begins, and time to respond may need adjustments. Once the data is analyzed, an instructor needs to examine the findings to identify in essence, what is and isn't working. For example, are the instructional methods effective? If not, what changes are merited and why? Instructional evaluation data is considered sensitive, and ethical standards for handling and sharing data must be maintained.

STATISTICAL DEMOGRAPHIC DIFFERENCES

The following section analyzes the statistical differences among a range of demographic variables of the instructors who completed the validation survey, including gender, age, geographic location, highest degree earned, and core teaching experience. While we have decades-old research demonstrating a relationship among instructor quality and learner achievement outcomes (Darling-Hammond, 2000), the relationship among instructor perceptions of competencies and related variables remains unexplored.

Demographic Differences Based on Gender

Analysis of variance for each core competency between male and female instructors in the sample did not illustrate many meaningful differences. Across the 19 competencies, five showed statistically significant differences between males and females at $\alpha = .05$ level. These competencies included competencies 1, 8, 9, 10, and 15:

- Competency 1—effective communication
- Competency 8—plan instructional approach
- Competency 9—plan of instructional resources
- Competency 10—preparation of instructional/learning activities
- Competency 15—retention and promotion of knowledge, skills, and attitudes

Across the five competencies, all the differences favored females with higher overall perceptions in each of the core instructor competencies. While research on an instructor's gender in relation to teaching quality or learner achievement has produced mixed findings (Collie et al., 2020; Sansone, 2017; Wagner et al., 2016), an instructor's gender continues to be an area of investigation, particularly in K–12 and higher education contexts.

Demographic Differences Based on Age

We examined four age categories inclusive of the age ranges from 20 to 39, 40 to 49, 50 to 59, and 60 and over. Readers can refer to Chapter 4 for the distributions across the age ranges. The analysis of variance across the age ranges showed that there were statistically significant differences on only two of the competencies at the $\alpha = .05$ level:

- Competency 7—specification of expected learning
- Competency 17—application of class management principles

After examining the contrasts from the post-hoc procedures, Competency 7 (specification of expected learning) showed differences between the 20 to 39 and 60 and over age ranges, and differences between the 50 to 59 and 60 and over age ranges. In both cases, the 60 and over age range held higher perceptions of this competency. With regards to Competency 17 (application of class management principles), we detected statistical differences between the 20 to 39 age group and the 60 and over age group. Again, the 60 and over age group showed overall higher scores on this instructor competency.

Demographic Differences Based on Geographic Location

The sample of participants was representative of both the United States and Canada ($n = 392$) and outside the United States and Canada ($n = 186$). Again, analysis of variance was employed to examine the differences between these two conditions at an $\alpha = .05$ level. In terms of geographic location, we detected differences on five of the core instructor competencies:

- Competency 1—effective communication
- Competency 4—ethical and legal standards
- Competency 14—learning promotion through feedback
- Competency 17—application of class management principles
- Competency 19—evaluation of instructional effectiveness

The results showed that for four of the competencies—1 (effective communication), 4 (ethical and legal standards), 14 (learning promotion through feedback), and 17 (application of class management principles)—instructors within the United States and Canada had higher overall perceptions for these core instructor competencies. However, instructors outside the

United States and Canada expressed higher perceptions for Competency 19 (evaluation of instructional effectiveness). Cross-country comparisons on instructor quality demonstrate that there are some major gaps between the United States and other developed nations on standardized assessments (Akiba et al., 2007). The instructor competencies between these developed nations warrant further investigation in the research literature.

Demographic Differences Based on Highest Degree Earned

Formal education can play an important role in how instructors perceive the importance of competencies that contribute to effective instructional practices (Angrist & Guryan, 2004). Here, we examined the instructors' highest degree earned (i.e., doctorate, masters, undergraduate, and other) in relation to the core instructor competencies. Again, employing the use of analysis of variance at an $\alpha = .05$ level, we detected statistically significant differences among education level and the core instructor competencies:

- Competency 14—learning promotion through feedback
- Competency 18—plan and preparation for monitoring and evaluating instruction

For Competency 14 (learning promotion through feedback), the contrasts only showed a difference between the perceptions of instructors possessing a doctoral degree and those with a master's degree in favor of those with a doctorate. Interestingly, the same difference was detected between instructors with doctoral degrees and those with master's degrees on Competency 18 (plan and preparation for monitoring and evaluating instruction), again with higher overall perceptions among instructors with a doctorate. Prior research has shown relationships between an instructor's education level and their ability to effectively integrate technology into their instruction (Liu et al., 2017; Ritzhaupt et al., 2012). Further, formal education and instructor professional development have been associated with instructor self-efficacy (Leino et al., 2022).

Demographic Differences Based on Core Teaching Experience

The final examination of statistical differences on the core instructor competencies is on the instructors' core teaching experiences as measured over time. The analyses compared instructors with no core teaching experience to those with less than five years of experience, those with 5 to 10 years of experience, and those with more than 10 years of experience. Using analysis of variance with an $\alpha = .05$ level, we did not detect statistical differences on any of the core instructor competencies based on core teaching experience as measured by time. While this finding is surprising, the research on years of teaching experience and measures of instructor quality has produced mixed results (Graham et al., 2020; Klassen & Chiu, 2010). Many individuals presume a straightforward linear relationship between teachers' years of experience and the quality of teaching; however, research demonstrates a much more complicated relationship among many important variables that "is non-linear and cyclical, whereby experience is one of many factors influencing the quality of teaching" (Graham et al., 2020, p. 2). Put simply, there are several factors that might contribute to an individual's perceptions of instructor competencies beyond years of experience.

SUMMARY

This chapter outlined the core competencies of instructors across demographic variables irrespective of instructional context (i.e., face-to-face, blended, or online). The IBSTPI instructor competencies and performance statements emerging in the core domain are intended to be important regardless of delivery methods and formats. The chapter provided supporting descriptions of each domain, competency, and performance statement and explored differences across demographic variables thought to moderate an instructor's perceptions of instructional competencies.

REFERENCES

Akiba, M., LeTendre, G. K., & Scribner, J. P. (2007). Teacher quality, opportunity gap, and national achievement in 46 countries. *Educational Researcher*, *36*(7), 369–387. https://doi.org/10.3102/0013189X07308739

Angrist, J. D., & Guryan, J. (2004). Teacher testing, teacher education, and teacher characteristics. *American Economic Review*, *94*(2), 241–246. https://doi.org/10.1257/0002828041302172

Collie, R. J., Bostwick, K. C., & Martin, A. J. (2020). Perceived autonomy support, relatedness with students, and workplace outcomes: An investigation of differences by teacher gender. *Educational Psychology*, *40*(3), 253–272. https://doi.org/10.1080/01443410.2019.1663791

Darling-Hammond, L. (2000). Teacher quality and student achievement. *Education Policy Analysis Archives*, *8*, 1–44. https://doi.org/10.14507/epaa.v8n1.2000

Dick, W., Carey, L., Carey, J. O. (2005). *The systematic design of instruction* (7th ed.). Pearson.

Graham, L. J., White, S. L., Cologon, K., & Pianta, R. C. (2020). Do teachers' years of experience make a difference in the quality of teaching? *Teaching and Teacher Education, 96*, 103190. https://doi.org/10.1016/j.tate.2020.103190

Halverson, L. R., & Graham, C. R. (2019). Learner engagement in blended learning environments: A conceptual framework. *Online Learning, 23*(2), 145–178. https://doi.org/10.24059/olj.v23i2.1481

Hattie, J. (2012). *Visible learning for teachers: Maximizing impact on learning.* Routledge.

Klassen, R. M., & Chiu, M. M. (2010). Effects on teachers' self-efficacy and job satisfaction: Teacher gender, years of experience, and job stress. *Journal of Educational Psychology, 102*(3), 741–756. https://doi.org/10.1037/a0019237

Leino, K., Nissinen, K., & Sirén, M. (2022). Associations between teacher quality, instructional quality and student reading outcomes in Nordic PIRLS 2016 data. *Large-scale Assessments in Education, 10*(1), 25. https://doi.org/10.1186/s40536-022-00146-4

Liu, F., Ritzhaupt, A. D., Dawson, K., & Barron, A. E. (2017). Explaining technology integration in K–12 classrooms: A multilevel path analysis model. *Educational Technology Research and Development, 65*, 795–813. https://doi.org/10.1007/s11423-016-9487-9

Mayer, R. E. (2002). Rote versus meaningful learning. *Theory Into Practice, 41*(4), 226–232. https://doi.org/10.1207/s15430421tip4104_4

Rajabalee, Y. B., & Santally, M. I. (2021). Learner satisfaction, engagement and performances in an online module: Implications for institutional e-learning policy. *Education and Information Technologies, 26*(3), 2623–2656. https://doi.org/10.1007/s10639-020-10375-1

Ritzhaupt, A. D., Dawson, K., & Cavanaugh, C. (2012). An investigation of factors influencing student use of technology in K–12 classrooms using path analysis. *Journal of Educational Computing Research, 46*(3), 229–254. https://doi.org/10.2190/EC.46.3.b

Sansone, D. (2017). Why does teacher gender matter? *Economics of Education Review, 61*, 9–18. https://doi.org/10.1016/j.econedurev.2017.09.004

Wagner, N., Rieger, M., & Voorvelt, K. (2016). Gender, ethnicity and teaching evaluations: Evidence from mixed teaching teams. *Economics of Education Review, 54*, 79–94. https://doi.org/10.1016/j.econedurev.2016.06.004

CHAPTER 6

COMPETENCIES FOR BLENDED TEACHING

CHAPTER OVERVIEW

This chapter focuses on competencies for blended teaching. The combining of face-to-face/offline instruction with virtual/online instruction is commonly called blended instruction, an approach noted for interactive and engaging learning. In this chapter, we provide the descriptive statistics for the competencies and performance statements that instructors consider critical for blended instruction. In addition, we discuss the differences based on instructor demographic characteristics (gender, age, geographic location, highest degree earned, blended teaching experience) in relation to the instructor competencies for blended teaching and learning.

Orienting Questions
- What competencies and performance statements do instructors consider critical for blended instruction?
- What instructor demographic characteristics (gender, age, geographic location, highest degree earned, blended teaching experience) are related to competencies for blended teaching and learning?

Blended Instruction

How one teaches competently and effectively in a blended setting is a topic undergoing continual development; an instructor who teaches in a blended setting is expected to continually learn, train, and adapt. Improving pedagogical practices and instructional strategies while effectively integrating offline and online instruction can be challenging for blended instructors. Thus, an instructor who aims to be effective in a blended setting must invest time to be technologically conversant and capable, coupled with the skills to provide a balanced blend to the overall course structure. Competent instructors in blended settings need to possess a variety of critical KSAs. On the IBSTPI Instructor Competencies questionnaire, there were 43 performance statements that were either adapted or written specifically for blended instruction. The blended instructors were asked to rate the competencies on a five-point Likert scale: *not critical* = 1, *slightly critical* = 2, *moderately critical* = 3, *critical* = 4, *highly critical* = 5.

Participants

Table 6.1 provides the demographic characteristics of the participants who completed the blended competencies section of the validation survey.

Foundations

1. Effective Communication

Paramount to an instructor's ability to effectively communicate in a blended setting is the capability to ensure coherence between offline and online communications. Instructors are tasked with making intentional decisions on when and why to use either traditional, offline communication means or online tools such as email, discussion boards, or text messages. Understanding the shortcomings, advantages, and evidence-based findings on offline and online means of communication is needed to effectively design and deliver blended instruction. Communicating online also requires an ability to select and appropriately use an array of symbols, emoticons, sounds, graphics, fonts, and other technology resources. By being consistent in the use of language, terminology, and tone, instructional messages will be coherent and inclusive. Table 6.2 shows the performance statements.

2. Improvement of Instructor Practices

Ensuring effective blended instruction requires instructors to employ technologies and tools to reflect, collaborate, and improve instructional

Competencies for Blended Teaching • 89

TABLE 6.1 Demographic Characteristics of the Blended Competencies Survey Participants

Demographic Variables	n	%
Gender		
Male	162	46.02%
Female	190	53.98%
Age Range		
20 to 39	76	18.77%
40 to 49	105	25.93%
50 to 59	139	34.32%
60 and over	85	20.99%
Geographic Location		
United States or Canada	288	70.94%
Outside the United States or Canada	118	29.06%
Educational Level		
Doctorate	122	30.05%
Master's Degree	144	35.47%
Undergraduate 2- or 4-year	61	15.02%
Other	79	19.46%
Blended Teaching Experience		
Less than 5 years	105	30.88%
5 to 10 years	93	27.35%
More than 10 years	142	41.76%

TABLE 6.2 Competencies Related to Effective Communication

Competency performance statements	N	M	SD
Core 1 Effective Communication	477	4.15	0.83
B1.a Use a combination of offline and online means of communication	481	3.97	1.057
B1.b Use technology features appropriately to communicate in respectful ways	480	4.21	0.876
B1.c Ensure consistency and coherence of messages across online and offline communications	481	4.29	0.927

practice. With today's technologies and tools, an instructor cannot stagnate, but instead needs to keep abreast of what is current and effective in order to actively use these tools and resources to share ideas with colleagues, seek expert advice, share what works/doesn't work, and so on. Creating a digital footprint through the use of a blog, for example, to share and collaborate

TABLE 6.3 Competencies Related to Improvement of Instructor Practices

Competency performance statements	N	M	SD
Core 2 Improvement of Instructor Practices	471	3.95	0.89
B2.a Use technologies and tools to collaborate with others	471	3.96	0.978
B2.b Collaborate with other educational technology professionals	472	3.94	0.968

with others to improve practice is a viable option. In some cases, improving blended practice is not as technologically dependent: Professional development can occur physically at a conference versus virtual attendance. Table 6.3 illustrates the performance statements.

3. Anticipation of Situational Factors

Blended learning can be implemented many ways but is most effective when it is designed intentionally with an awareness of the blended environment and its impact on learning. An instructor needs to figure out how the tools and technologies will support the process of learning and create the online and offline means for learners to achieve sufficient time on task. Instructors will need to address questions like, "What are the different types of technologies available, and are these technologies compatible?" and "What kinds of technology support and access are needed?" Table 6.4 shows the performance statements.

4. Ethical and Legal Standards

Protecting intellectual property (IP) rights is challenging, and yet instructors blending offline and online resources must do what they can to prevent IP rights violations. All instructional materials (e.g., lectures, discussions, videos, blogs, and assessments) are subject to copyright protection, and there are multiple preventative measures an instructor may need

TABLE 6.4 Competencies Related to Anticipation of Situational Factors

Competency performance statements	N	M	SD
Core 3 Anticipation of Situational Factors	460	3.78	0.99
B3.a Specify how online and offline technologies and tools are integrated	461	3.69	1.102
B3.b Identify online and offline technology and tool issues that may impact learning and performance	461	3.87	1.026
B3.c Identify implications of converting to blended instruction	460	3.79	1.101

TABLE 6.5 Competencies Related to Ethical and Legal Standards

Competency performance statements	N	M	SD
Core 4 Ethical and Legal Standards	454	4.51	0.72
B4.a Ensure respect of online and offline intellectual property rights	455	4.51	0.771
B4.b Recognize and deter online and offline situations that violate privacy rights	455	4.51	0.742

to take. For example, an instructor is expected to monitor and maintain indications of use of others' property, abide by the laws of their country (i.e., fair use laws in the United States), and prevent compromises of academic integrity. Table 6.5 shows the performance statements.

5. Establishment of Professionalism

Given that blended learning integrates technology to enhance learning, those who instruct using blended methods need to be competent users of technologies and tools. With the fast pace of technological change come new tools and opportunities that a professional instructor must review and adopt, if appropriate. A basic understanding of a computer's physical components (e.g., hardware) and its software (e.g., operating system updates) is a must, as is keeping current on the interoperability of the technologies. Learning may involve a range of options including, for example, tablets, wearable technology, virtual reality devices, and social media; thus, an instructor must be capable of not only using these devices, but also assuring that these options are pedagogically appropriate. Blended instructors demonstrate professionalism by setting the same behavioral standards across delivery modes; instructors should begin traditional instruction on time and should also begin online synchronous activities on time. By setting clear and consistent behaviors and attitudes, instructors using blended methods promote learner engagement and encourage self-directed learning. Table 6.6 shows the performance statements.

TABLE 6.6 Competencies Related to Establishment of Professionalism

Competency performance statements	N	M	SD
Core 5 Establishment of Professionalism	437	4.13	0.79
B5.a Keep current on new technologies and tools and their pedagogical uses in online and offline contexts	440	4.07	0.926
B5.b Demonstrate proficiencies for using technologies and tools in teaching and learning	439	4.14	0.86
B5.c Demonstrate consistent behaviors and attitudes in online and offline contexts	439	4.18	0.921

6. Management of Instructional Resources

Managing blended learning requires an instructor to be competent in designing learning activities that are both offline and online. An instructor first plans the instruction and organization of it, but much more is required, for one needs to organize, coordinate, store, transmit, and protect the instructional elements and resources. How will instructional data be accessed? Via a digital folder system, for example? All instructional materials need to be secured and protected, and an instructor is to oversee and consistently manage these resources. Table 6.7 illustrates the performance statements.

Designing for Learning

7. Specification of Expected Learning

Quality blended learning is not a result when digital versions of offline learning resources shared in traditional settings are transferred to online settings. A blended instructor must select instructional content and delivery format that best suit either offline or online learning and explicitly inform learners how the instruction is organized, located, and scheduled. Learners also need to know why and how a particular technology will support learning. For example, an online blog promotes collaborative thinking and sharing versus the use of an individual paper submission. It is imperative that blended learning is coherently designed; learning objectives are not developed separately for any offline or online setting, but rather are developed to advance learning and support appropriate usages of technology to enable learning. Table 6.8 shows the performance statements.

TABLE 6.7 Competencies Related to Management of Instructional Resources

Competency performance statements	N	M	SD
Core 6 Management of Instructional Resources	434	3.69	1.03
B6.a Coordinate online and offline instructional resources	435	3.72	1.048
B6.b Use online and offline technologies and tools to manage instructional resources	435	3.65	1.097

TABLE 6.8 Competencies Related to Specification of Expected Learning

Competency performance statements	N	M	SD
Core 7 Specification of Expected Learning	432	4.04	0.87
B7.a Select types of content for online and offline learning	433	4.07	0.979
B7.b Specify how technologies are used to support learning and performance	434	3.82	1.042
B7.c Ensure learning objectives are consistent in online and offline settings	434	4.23	0.979

8. Plan of Instructional Approach

Designing instructional content for blended delivery requires a focus on learner engagement that effectively integrates offline and online instructional and learning activities. Essentially, an instructor needs to explore instructional modalities and delivery media (e.g., tools and technologies) and learning activities. By doing so, an instructor is able to capitalize on the strengths of both offline and online learning modalities and activities. Table 6.9 shows the performance statements.

9. Plan of Instructional Resources

Blended instructors, like all who plan instruction, must plan for instruction that is focused on the learner and not just the content. In blended settings, not only are learning objectives fundamental to designing effective instruction, but instructional strategies and learner preferences are also front and center during instructional planning. Blended learning involves conceptualizing approaches to combine the "fragmented" offline and online instructional elements into effective blended learning. Table 6.10 illustrates the performance statements.

10. Preparation of Instructional/Learning Activities

Blended instructors need to design learning so that a learner's user experience is simple and logical. It is essential that an instructor be deliberate and organized when linking offline and online learning activities. For example, an in-class discussion could be continued with an online discussion. It is never wise to make assumptions about learners, and when it comes to learners' technical readiness, a blended instructor must anticipate that directions and support for the learners are needed. Table 6.11 shows the performance statements.

TABLE 6.9 Competencies Related to Plan of Instructional Approach

Competency performance statements	N	M	SD
Core 8 Plan of Instructional Approach	428	3.92	0.94
B8.a Integrate online and offline learning and performance strategies	429	4.08	0.98
B8.b Identify online and offline activities	431	3.76	1.041

TABLE 6.10 Competencies Related to Plan of Instructional Resources

Competency performance statements	N	M	SD
Core 9 Plan of Instructional Resources	428	4.04	0.85
B9.a Select the optimal combination of resources	429	4.02	0.903
B9.b Integrate resources into blended lessons	428	4.06	0.91

TABLE 6.11 Competencies Related to Preparation of Instructional/Learning Activities

Competency performance statements	N	M	SD
Core 10 Preparation of Instructional/Learning Activities	427	3.87	1
B10.a Prepare effective transitions between online and offline activities	429	3.84	1.057
B10.b Provide support for learners to attain technical readiness for online and offline settings	427	3.89	1.069

11. Preparation of Assessment and Feedback

Assessment and feedback best practices apply no matter the instructional setting, but with blended approaches, an instructor must consider how to support learning through the use of technology and tools. These considerations can include hardware (e.g., computer, mobile device), software (e.g., online testing), and issues such as platform compatibility. Along with selecting appropriate tools and technologies, a blended instructor will decide why and when assessment and feedback are provided. All learning assessments (i.e., formative and summative) must be compliant with accessibility guidelines and policies. In particular, the use of digital assessments may prompt a blended instructor to seek guidance and support. Learners will need clear information on how to effectively locate and complete all assessments and may need additional assistance in knowing how to access and use digital measures. Additionally, a blended instructor will need to plan for clear, effective, and ongoing learner feedback in both the online and offline settings. Table 6.12 illustrates the performance statements and associated statistics.

TABLE 6.12 Competencies Related to Preparation of Assessment and Feedback

Competency performance statements	N	M	SD
Core 11 Preparation of Assessment and Feedback	417	3.71	1.02
B11.a Identify online and offline technologies and tools for assessment and feedback	419	3.77	1.097
B11.b Justify each online and offline technology used for assessment and feedback	421	3.47	1.247
B11.c Use digital and non-digital tools to create assessments	420	3.6	1.198
B11.d Prepare instructions describing online and offline assessments	421	3.85	1.117
B11.e Prepare feedback strategies for online and offline settings	421	3.83	1.149

Facilitating Learning

12. Learner Engagement

Engagement is critical to effective teaching and learning processes, and blended instructors need to engage learners through the use of technologies in physical settings (e.g., electronic whiteboards) and virtual settings (e.g., digital cameras). It can be challenging, however, to select the right technologies and tools to engage learners. Instructors need to first focus on learning and then use appropriate technologies that allow learners to construct understanding. Blended learners need access to content and resources, but learning includes many activities, such as practice, collaboration, and questioning, that can be effectively achieved through the use of technologies and tools. Throughout a learning cycle, tools and technology are also used to support instructional processes, from assessing learner prerequisite knowledge to facilitating synthesis and summaries. A blended instructor is expected to effectively integrate the technology and tools throughout any instruction. Table 6.13 illustrates the statistics and associated performance statements.

13. Instruction Adaptation to Learners/Learning Environment

Group dynamics—the roles and behaviors of individuals that influence group members and the group as a whole—impact the learning process. In a blended environment, instructors need to match the grouping strategy with the objectives and be prepared for virtual group dynamics that may require more commitment and effort on the part of an instructor. A blended instructor can monitor group dynamics, for example, by extending content and learning time in times of confusion or inactivity. Instructors need to be flexible and adaptive by adjusting digital tools as learner needs arise and in order to promote effective group interactions and collaborations. Table 6.14 shows the performance statements and descriptive statistics.

татБЛЕ 6.13 Competencies Related to Learner Engagement

Competency performance statements	N	M	SD
Core 12 Learner Engagement	436	3.99	0.9
B12.a Use technologies and tools to engage and motivate learners	439	4.08	0.967
B12.b Use technologies and tools to assist in bringing a lesson to closure	437	3.93	1.033
B12.c Transition seamlessly between technology and non-technology strategies	438	3.98	1.029

TABLE 6.14 Competencies Related to Instruction Adaptation to Learners/Learning Environment

Competency performance statements	N	M	SD
Core 13 Instruction Adaptation to Learners/Learning Environment	436	3.93	0.92
B13.a Adjust the use of tools based on online and offline group dynamics	436	3.97	1.055

14. Learning Promotion Through Feedback

In blended settings, instructors will provide offline and online feedback to learners. For the feedback to be effective, a blended instructor will need to describe and demonstrate where and how feedback will be given. Blended learner feedback can be offered in a variety of ways and can range from automated responses to written, verbal, and visual feedback. A blended instructor will make it clear how all types of feedback (self, peer, or instructor) can be accessed and how to use any digital tools (e.g., classroom response system). Table 6.15 illustrates the performance statements and associated statistics.

15. Retention and Promotion of Knowledge, Skills, and Attitudes

A blended environment can be rich with opportunities for learners, and a blended instructor must be selective when it comes to how to best facilitate learning. An instructor will need to select appropriate technologies for use in both offline and online settings that encourage learners to express thinking through multiple avenues and tools such as offline and online discussions, shared drafts, and synthesis of ideas. Learners can, for example, begin synthesizing ideas using a concept map that can be created offline or online. A blended instructor can promote both individual and group attainment of KSAs through the use of individual journals or group posted debriefings. Table 6.16 shows the performance statements and statistics.

TABLE 6.15 Competencies Related to Learning Promotion Through Feedback

Competency performance statements	N	M	SD
Core 14 Learning Promotion through Feedback	434	3.93	0.92
B14.a Instruct learners on feedback mechanisms in online and offline contexts	435	3.96	0.998
B14.b Enable learners to provide peer feedback using online and offline tools and strategies	435	3.88	1.051
B14.c Provide learners with feedback using online and offline tools and strategies	436	3.94	1.053

TABLE 6.16 Competencies Related to Retention and Promotion of Knowledge, Skills, and Attitudes

Competency performance statements	N	M	SD
Core 15 Retention and Promotion of KSAs	430	4.16	0.94
B15.a. Engage learners in expressing knowledge, skills, and attitudes in online and offline contexts	430	4.16	0.942

16. Transfer of Learned KSAs to Other Contexts

Well-designed and well-delivered blended instruction tends to be well-organized and flexible. Those two variables, along with a blended instructor's know-how in building upon the strengths of offline and online formats, will promote learners' transfer of KSAs. A blended instructor can use technology-infused tools to encourage learners to explore and demonstrate applications of learning that may include social media, visualization tools, and virtual fields. Table 6.17 illustrates the statistics and associated performance statements.

17. Application of Class Management Principles

In all learning settings, instructors need to clarify and set clear expectations for learner behaviors. Those who instruct in blended settings must consider the complexity of a "dual learning environment" and therefore must provide learners comprehensive guidance. In order to effectively manage blended learning, instructors are expected to guide students using a variety of tactics. For example, they will need to specify where participation is expected both offline or online and to promote learners' time management skills (e.g., discussion posting policies on timing, protocol, etc.). Table 6.18 shows the performance statements.

TABLE 6.17 Competencies Related to Transfer of Learned KSAs to Other Contexts

Competency performance statements	N	M	SD
Core 16 Transfer of Learned KSAs to Other Contexts	425	4.18	0.93
B16.a Stimulate application of learning beyond instructional context using online and offline tools and strategies	425	4.18	0.925

TABLE 6.18 Competencies Related to Application of Class Management Principles

Competency performance statements	N	M	SD
Core 17 Application of Class Management Principles	425	3.90	1
B17.a Use online and offline tools and strategies to manage learner behavior	426	3.96	1.006

Evaluating Learning

18. Plan and Preparation for Monitoring and Evaluating Instruction

Evaluating blended learning instruction involves three distinctly important factors: pedagogical, learner needs, and technology integration. An instructor must plan for a variety of complementary evaluation strategies to ascertain what is and is not working effectively in a blended environment. Evaluations and reviews can be completed by multiple stakeholders, such as the learners, peer instructors, or administrators. Through the use of formative online or offline evaluation measures, an instructor is able to modify as deemed necessary based on learner insights. Summative measures to evaluate blended instruction are also needed, and as with the formative evaluations, an instructor needs to provide context and directions for the evaluation activities and to emphasize the value of stakeholders' input in evaluating instruction. Table 6.19 shows the performance statements and associated statistics.

19. Evaluation of Instructional Effectiveness

Evaluation findings have the potential to improve and validate instructional effectiveness, but interpreting the findings can be challenging. An instructor in a blended setting will need to utilize an organized approach to best compile and analyze evaluations. By using a clear approach, an instructor will be able to make distinctions as to which factor (i.e., pedagogical, learner needs, and technology integration) needs adjusting, as well as being able to identify patterns across the responses. Table 6.20 shows the performance statements.

TABLE 6.19 Competencies Related to Plan and Preparation for Monitoring and Evaluating Instruction

Competency performance statements	N	M	SD
Core 18 Plan and Preparation for Monitoring and Evaluating Instruction	425	3.74	1.06
B18.a Plan corresponding evaluation for online and offline delivery	427	3.74	1.124
B18.b Identify online and offline strategies for evaluating the effectiveness of blending instruction	427	3.69	1.157
B18.c Prepare directions for online and offline evaluation activities	426	3.82	1.102

TABLE 6.20 Competencies Related to Evaluation of Instructional Effectiveness

Competency performance statements	N	M	SD
Core 19 Evaluation of Instructional Effectiveness	426	3.91	1.07
B19.a Compile and analyze evaluation findings from both online and offline settings	426	3.91	1.074

STATISTICAL DEMOGRAPHIC DIFFERENCES

Differences Based on Gender

Among the instructors who reported their gender, 162 instructors identified as male and 190 instructors identified as female. Among the 19 competencies, male and female instructors significantly differed in their perception of 17 blended competencies at the $p < .05$ level. The female instructors considered these competencies as more critical than the male instructors. Only Competency 2 (improvement of instructor practices) and Competency 13 (instruction adaptation to learners/learning environment) did not indicate significant difference between male and female instructors.

For now, limited evidence supporting or refuting gender differences in perceptions of blended learning instructor competencies is available. A study using student teachers found that males reported more learning satisfaction when taught via blended learning and surmised this was due to more interest in technology by males (Cobanoglu, 2018). Empirical evidence of gender differences, however, in instructor readiness for teaching with technology has been an ongoing topic of interest (Cai et al., 2017; Qazi et al., 2022). While currently limited in scope, findings on how prepared instructors consider themselves for blended instruction do exist. Garrison and Vaughan (2013) report that the lack of adequate technical preparation can result in instructors merely replicating traditional instructional methods instead of implementing blended learning methods, along with harboring fewer positive attitudes towards blended instruction. There is research indicating gender differences in the use of technology in blended learning, with male instructors possessing more advanced technology skills (Moukali, 2012), but no significant differences were found between genders' attitudes toward implementing blending instruction (Villalon, 2018).

Differences Based on Age

Among the instructors who provided their age, there were 76 instructors in the 20- to 39-years age range, 105 instructors between 40 to 49 years, 139 instructors between 50 to 59 years, and 85 instructors above 60 years. Among the 19 competencies, instructors had no age-related significant differences on the blended competencies at the $p < .05$ level.

Differences Based on Geographic Location

Among the instructors who provided their geographic location, 288 were in the United States or Canada, and 118 were outside of the United

States and Canada. Based on their geographic location, instructors significantly differed in their perception on 12 of the 19 competencies at the $p < .05$ level. Significant differences were found between respondents for 12 competencies: 2, 3, 6, 7, 8, 10, 11, 12, 14, 15, 18, 19. Those outside the United States or Canada rated these competencies as more critical than those within the United States or Canada.

Empirical evidence that could provide insights on factors influencing the survey respondents to differ based on geographic location is hard to pinpoint. Across the globe, however, there are different models in use to define and guide instructor competencies. Thus, the relative importance of a specific instructor competency is related to the contextual vantage point an instructor possesses. For example, a study of preservice geography teachers' professional competencies found that the competencies the teachers found to be very important reflected the types of thinking central to German geographic education (Ammoneit et al., 2022). Another perspective comes from a study by Belmont et al. (2019), who found that multicultural environments (in their case, flipped classrooms in cross-border contexts) prompt instructors to focus attention on diversity. While the IBSTPI survey did not directly explore perspectives related to diversity, their impact across geographic locations is one that merits further review.

Differences Based on Highest Degree Earned

Among the participants who provided their highest degree earned, 122 instructors had earned a doctoral degree, 144 instructors had earned a master's degree, 61 instructors had earned an undergraduate 2- or 4-year degree, and 79 instructors had earned other degrees. Among the 19 competencies, based on highest degree earned, instructors had no significant differences on the blended competencies at the $p < .05$ level.

Differences Based on Blended Teaching Experience

Among the instructors who provided their blended teaching experience, there were 17 instructors who had no years of experience, 105 instructors who had less than 5 years of experience, 93 instructors who had 5 to 10 years of experience, and 142 instructors who had more than 10 years of experience. Analysis of variance showed significant differences were found between respondents for Competency 1 and Competency 6. However, Tukey post hoc analysis showed differences only for Competency 6, between those with no experience and those with 10 or more years of experience for blended instructional delivery. Those with more years of experience rated that competency as more critical.

SUMMARY

This chapter provided the descriptive statistics of competencies and performance statements that instructors consider critical for blended teaching and learning along with explanations describing how the performance statements reflect blended instruction planning and delivery. In addition, we discuss significant differences based on instructor demographic characteristics (gender, age, geographic location, highest degree earned, and blended instructional experience); with blended instruction, only gender and geographic location demographics were found to reveal significant differences in the respondent's perception of the level of criticality of for blended instruction.

REFERENCES

Ammoneit, R., Turek, A., & Peter, C. (2022). Pre-service geography teachers' professional competencies in education for sustainable development. *Education Sciences, 12,* 1–20. https://doi.org/10.3390/educsci12010042

Belmont, J., Sanchez, S., & del Pino Espejo, M. (2019). Projection of the flipped learning methodology in the teaching staff of cross-border contexts. *Journal of New Approaches in Educational Research, 8(2),* 184–200. https://eric.ed.gov/?id=EJ1223117

Cai, Z., Fan, X., & Du, J. (2017). Gender and attitudes toward technology use: A meta-analysis. *Computers & Education, 105,* 1–13. https://doi.org/10.1016/j.compedu.2016.11.003

Cobanoglu, A. (2018). Student teachers' satisfaction for blended learning via Edmodo learning. *Behavior and Information Technology, 37(2),* 133–144. https://doi.org/10.1080/0144929X.2017.1417481

Garrison, R., & Vaughan, N. (2013). Institutional change and leadership associated with blended learning innovation: Two case studies. *The Internet and Higher Education, 18,* 24–28. https://doi.org/10.1016/j.iheduc.2012.09.001

Moukali, K. H. (2012). *Factors that affect faculty attitudes toward adoption of technology-rich blended learning* [Doctoral dissertation, University of Kansas]. https://eric.ed.gov/?id=ED551362

Qazi, A., Hasan, N., Abayomi-Alli, O., Hardaker, G., Scherer, R., Sarker, Y., Sanjoy, P., & Maitama, J. (2022). Gender differences in information and communication technology use & skills: A systematic review and meta-analysis. *Education and Information Technologies, 27,* 4225–4258. https://doi.org/10.1007/s10639-021-10775-x

Villalon, C. (2018). Influence of instructors' attitudes, gender and technology training when implement blended learning. *American Society for Clinical Laboratory Science, 31(2),* 111. https://doi.org/10.29074/ascls.2018000984

CHAPTER 7

COMPETENCIES FOR ONLINE TEACHING

CHAPTER OVERVIEW

This chapter focuses on competencies for Internet-based online teaching that offers "thoughtfully designed, quality, student-focused learning experiences, built on proven best practices that create effective interactions between learners, peers, instructors, and content" (Mathes, 2020, para. 5). We provide the descriptive statistics of competencies and performance statements that instructors consider critical for online teaching, along with explanations describing how the performance statements reflect online instruction and delivery. In addition, we discuss the differences based on instructor demographic characteristics (gender, age, geographic location, highest degree earned, online teaching experience) in relation to the online instructor competencies.

Orienting Questions

- What competencies and performance statements do instructors consider critical for online teaching?
- What instructor demographic characteristics (gender, age, geographic location, highest degree earned, online teaching experience) are related to competencies for online teaching?

Instructor Competencies, pages 103–120
Copyright © 2023 by Information Age Publishing
www.infoagepub.com
All rights of reproduction in any form reserved.

ONLINE INSTRUCTION

In many instructional settings across the globe, the use of instructional technologies and the availability of online learning opportunities are expanding. Competencies to teach online are different from competencies required to teach face-to-face, as the strategies and technologies used in online instruction are different from teaching in person. An instructor who aims to be effective in an online setting must be technologically and pedagogically competent. Hence, competencies for online instructional delivery and research validating these competencies are needed. There were 44 competencies that were either adapted or written specifically for online delivery focusing on the synchronous and asynchronous modalities. The online instructors were asked to rate the competencies on a five-point Likert scale: *not critical* = 1, *slightly critical* = 2, *moderately critical* = 3, *critical* = 4, *highly critical* = 5.

Participants

Table 7.1 provides the demographic characteristics of the participants who completed the online competencies section of the validation survey.

Foundations

1. Effective Communication
To communicate effectively is an important life skill in any situation, but when it comes to online instruction, instructors have to adapt to effectively communicate with the learners. In fully online settings, when instructor and learner are physically separated, instructors are challenged to increase the interactivity of the teaching and learning process through the use of digital tools and pedagogical competence. The five performance statements to communicate effectively were deemed critical by the respondents; teaching online requires communicating synchronously and asynchronously through a variety of approaches (e.g., email, discussion boards, social media, video conferencing platforms) while facilitating and modeling appropriate decorum, courtesy, and respect of learners' time and technical abilities/possibilities. In instructional settings without walls, so to speak, instructors need to avoid ambiguity and employ a cultural perspective to ensure that all learners receive the same message. Table 7.2 includes performance statements and descriptive statistics

2. Improvement of Instructor Practices
All instructors can improve, and a common pathway to doing so is via a community. For those who instruct online and are often physically separated from colleagues or other support systems, they must actively use

TABLE 7.1 Demographic Characteristics of the Online Competencies Survey Participants

Demographic Variables	n	%
Gender		
Male	162	46.02%
Female	190	53.98%
Age Range		
20 to 39	76	18.77%
40 to 49	105	25.93%
50 to 59	139	34.32%
60 and over	85	20.99%
Geographic Location		
United States or Canada	288	70.94%
Outside the U.S. or Canada	118	29.06%
Educational Level		
Doctorate	122	30.05%
Master's Degree	144	35.47%
Undergraduate 2- or 4-year	61	15.02%
Other	79	19.46%
Face-to-Face Teaching Experience		
Less than 5 years	131	41.19%
5 to 10 years	83	26.10%
More than 10 years	104	32.70%

TABLE 7.2 Competencies Related to Effective Communication

Competency performance statements	N	M	SD
Core 1 Effective Communication	470	4.22	0.80
OL1.a Use online means to communicate	473	4.02	1.023
OL1.b Ensure respectful interactions in online synchronous and asynchronous communications	473	4.37	0.892
OL1.c Ensure consistency and coherence of messages across synchronous and asynchronous communications	474	4.27	0.915
OL1.d Ensure timely synchronous and asynchronous exchanges	474	4.24	0.903
OL1.e Adopt a cultural communication perspective	474	4.20	0.985

technology tools and methods to connect with other professionals to share ideas, seek advice, request faculty development, discuss what works/doesn't work, and so on. An online instructor who is open to learning from other

106 • Instructor Competencies

TABLE 7.3 Competencies Related to Improvement of Instructor Practices

Competency performance statements	N	M	SD
Core 2 Improvement of Instructor Practices	464	3.80	1
OL2.a Use online technologies and tools to collaborate with others	464	3.81	1.033
OL2.b Collaborate with other online instructional professionals	464	3.80	1.095

professionals, as well as from students, is better able to adapt to these dynamic learning environments and to feel comfortable with online tools and technologies. Collaboration is a key to growth and development of online instructors' pedagogical and technical know-how because of the multitude of skills needed and the evolving nature of online teaching and learning. Table 7.3 includes performance statements and descriptive statistics.

3. Anticipation of Situational Factors

Instruction is designed to be purposeful in supporting and engaging learning, but it can be impacted by needs and situational factors. Online instruction is dependent on technology, and with that come issues, such as availability of types of technologies or platform compatibility. A competent instructor is expected to address these types of issues, but the expectation isn't that online instructors are to be all-knowing when it comes to today's technologies and tools. Being open and curious to the myriad of online tools and technologies facilitates effective online instruction, as does this premise: design instruction for online. Merely converting traditional instruction into online delivery is insufficient; effective online instruction instead requires design modifications and the use of specific online strategies and interactions. Table 7.4 includes performance statements and descriptive statistics.

4. Ethical and Legal Standards

All instructors are expected to demonstrate personal integrity and maintain a high degree of ethical conduct. While no specific ethics instructions

TABLE 7.4 Competencies Related to Anticipation of Situational Factors

Competency performance statements	N	M	SD
Core 3 Anticipation of Situational Factors	452	3.92	0.98
OL3.a Identify online technology and tool issues that may impact learning, and performance	453	3.95	1.023
OL3.b Identify implications of converting to online instruction	453	3.90	1.092

are provided to clarify what to do, or when and how to do it, ethical principles provide a framework for instructors to use when making decisions. All instructors make ethical judgments, and for those who teach online with environments that cross physical and cultural boundaries, additional ethical demands are placed on instructors. In particular, privacy and property rights are paramount when working with online and offline intellectual property delivered via multimedia. Online instructors are to ensure that attribution of others' property is properly provided, as well as actions being taken to prevent and detect plagiarism through monitoring and the use of tools such as plagiarism detection software. When it comes to protecting privacy rights of all (i.e., learners, colleagues, or guests), instructors must recognize that all learner information belongs to the learner and is to be kept private. In doing so, online instructors are responsible for implementing best practices to keep data private and secure not only for students, but for others, such as a guest speaker. A confidentiality agreement might be necessary, and if anyone is to be recorded, they need to be informed first. It is an imperative for online instructors to keep current on these issues and to develop good Internet practices to protect not only their learners, but their own privacy and intellectual property. Table 7.5 includes performance statements and descriptive statistics.

5. Establishment of Professionalism

Online instructional environments evolve due to the rapid pace of technological change, and it is imperative that online instructors keep current and informed about online technologies and tools to find the best solutions for effective teaching and learning. Instructors are tasked not only with engaging learners through the use of pedagogical strategies and technology, but also with staying up-to-date on innovative and appropriate online tools and technologies to effectively manage instructional resources. Instructing generally does not require an individual to be well-versed in all aspects of online tools and environments, but a "never stop learning" mindset is needed to assess emerging technologies, be open to new approaches, and maintain a basic familiarity with existing tools' and technologies' capabilities. Table 7.6 includes performance statements and descriptive statistics.

TABLE 7.5 Competencies Related to Ethical and Legal Standards			
Competency performance statements	N	M	SD
Core 4 Ethical and Legal Standards	447	4.52	0.74
OL4.a Ensure respect of online intellectual property rights	447	4.51	0.754
OL4.b Recognize and deter online situations that violate privacy rights	448	4.52	0.774

108 ▪ Instructor Competencies

TABLE 7.6 Competencies Related to Establishment of Professionalism

Competency performance statements	N	M	SD
Core 5 Establishment of Professionalism	431	4.12	0.85
OL5.a Keep current on new technologies and tools and their pedagogical uses in online environments	433	4.08	0.963
OL5.b Demonstrate proficiencies for using technologies and tools in online teaching and learning	433	4.10	0.903
OL5.c Demonstrate consistent behaviors and attitudes in synchronous and asynchronous contexts	433	4.18	0.937

6. Management of Instructional Resources

Online instructors are in dynamic environments that demand refining and learning a mix of skills. These instructors need to be technically proficient, but not necessarily technically advanced. By possessing adequate technological skills, they are able to be proficient at organizing, storing, accessing, sharing, and protecting instructional content and resources through the use of various online resources such as course management systems, data repositories, and digital file systems. Online instructors will need to be aware of the latest updates and manage instructional materials by updating, removing previous learning information, or other modifications as needed. Table 7.7 includes performance statements and descriptive statistics.

Designing for Learning

7. Specification of Expected Learning

Effective instruction begins by figuring out what a learner will be able to know and do as a result of instruction. Online instructional planning begins with the end in mind but also requires an instructor to address how learners will engage with the content, each other, and the instructor. In traditional/conventional instructional settings, instructors and learners can interact in real-time and use visual and verbal cues. Online instruction, however, may be delivered synchronously, asynchronously, or as a mixture, and instructors' approaches to clarifying materials and providing feedback

TABLE 7.7 Competencies Related to Management of Instructional Resources

Competency performance statements	N	M	SD
Core 6 Management of Instructional Resources	427	3.74	1.01
OL6.a Use online technologies and tools to manage instructional resources	429	3.69	1.09
OL6.b Manage versions of online instructional material	427	3.78	1.085

require clear and targeted communication via multiple channels. An instructor's pedagogical practices need to be effective and consistent no matter the context, but online instruction has unique aspects. For example, interactions in real time allow for live interchanges between instructor and learner with opportunities to provide responsive exchanges such as just-in-time feedback. Asynchronous interactions, however, are delayed, but instructors still need to provide effective and timely feedback. Table 7.8 includes performance statements and descriptive statistics.

8. Plan of Instructional Approach

All effective instruction requires selecting appropriate strategies to promote learning and performance, but when it comes to online instructional planning, there are some unique considerations to be addressed. Planning for online instruction involves considering how the online environment can support the learning objectives, leveraging technology to engage learners, and providing digital tools and resources to facilitate learning. Instructors have access to a variety of interactive methodologies appropriate for traditional instruction and online instruction, but they must also be knowledgeable of the digital tools that support these strategies. Instructors need to identify tools and resources that support a myriad of approaches such as peer-to-peer interactions, learner presentations, and simulations. Integral to planning for instructional strategies is the planning to support online assessment for and of learning. Instructors need to select from a variety of tools available for alternative forms of assessments (i.e., projects, concept maps, and oral testing) and for more standard forms of assessments (i.e., examinations, quizzes, and essays), as well as timely feedback (automated and non-automated). Table 7.9 includes performance statements and descriptive statistics.

TABLE 7.8 Competencies Related to Specification of Expected Learning

Competency performance statements	N	M	SD
Core 7 Specification of Expected Learning	425	3.95	0.99
OL7.a Determine the learning process for synchronous or asynchronous activities	427	3.93	1.029
OL7.b Determine learning objectives for synchronous and/or asynchronous activities	425	3.96	1.022

TABLE 7.9 Competencies Related to Plan of Instructional Approach

Competency performance statements	N	M	SD
Core 8 Plan of Instructional Approach	421	3.90	0.98
OL8.a Integrate online learning and performance strategies	423	4.08	1.025
OL8.b Identify online and offline activities	422	3.73	1.107

9. Plan of Instructional Resources

Online instruction requires ample preparation to allow for thorough instructional design and for developing and creating the virtual materials/courses. Instructors need to locate online resources, collaborators, and experts to support and enrich learning. Specific tasks may include identifying examples, data, anecdotes, visuals, and other multimedia and integrating these resources appropriately. Table 7.10 includes performance statements and descriptive statistics.

10. Preparation of Instructional/Learning Activities

Prior to actual instruction, an online instructor is using technology and tools to create, prepare, and pilot-test instructional resources for online delivery. They will need to also consider and prepare for support resources to ensure their learners either have or can attain online technical readiness skills. Some learners may also need guidance on how to learn online, and, for example, advice on practicing good time management skills or utilizing effective study techniques is helpful. Given that online learning is offered in different modes (i.e., synchronous and asynchronous, collaboratively and individually), an instructor needs to plan for clear transitions to facilitate learning and to provide an accessible and organized learning environment. When instructors use effective design and aesthetics, they are able to create online learning experiences with logical navigability along with easy-to-locate instructions and directions. Table 7.11 includes performance statements and descriptive statistics.

TABLE 7.10 Competencies Related to Plan of Instructional Resources

Competency performance statements	N	M	SD
Core 9 Plan of Instructional Resources	421	3.88	0.96
OL.9.a Select a combination of online resources	422	3.78	1.024
OL.9.b Integrate resources to online lessons	421	3.99	0.996

TABLE 7.11 Competencies Related to Preparation of Instructional/Learning Activities

Competency performance statements	N	M	SD
Core 10 Preparation of Instructional/Learning Activities	418	3.91	0.99
OL.10.a Provide support for learners to attain technical readiness for online settings	420	3.87	1.119
OL.10.b Prepare effective transitions among online learning activities	419	3.85	1.085
OL.10.c Organize resources and activities in online settings	421	4.02	1.029

11. Preparation of Assessment and Feedback

When preparing to assess student learning and performance online, an understanding of what is technically feasible is essential. Online instructors may need to select the hardware, prepare for different types of devices (e.g., tablet or PC), and consider compatibility issues. In some settings, however, instructors select from the assessment tools that are supported by their employer to create a variety of secure online assessment methods. Online instructors have access to a variety of features in online assessment tools, and they need to learn how to use these tools and prepare their students to effectively complete the assessments. Effective online assessment is integrated throughout instruction, and an instructor will be responsible for an assessment response strategy. In some cases, feedback can be automated, but in other instances, an instructor will determine in advance of instruction such variables as the expected rate of instructor turnaround response time, whether learners will receive individual or collective feedback, or whether there will be peer-to-peer feedback. Table 7.12 includes performance statements and descriptive statistics.

Facilitating Learning

12. Learner Engagement

Online instructors can use many of the strategies from traditional settings to engage learners, but they must also become versed in digital tool options. Undoubtedly, selecting the right digital tools first depends on how the tools connect to learning and how pedagogy will inform these decisions. Instructors will need to review and select online resources (i.e., apps, software, social media, blogs, Twitter) and supportive peripherals (i.e., digital

TABLE 7.12 Competencies Related to Preparation of Assessment and Feedback

Competency performance statements	N	M	SD
Core 11 Preparation of Assessment and Feedback	410	3.72	1.05
OL11.a Identify technologies and digital tools for online assessment and feedback	414	3.75	1.153
OL11.b Justify each online technology used for assessment and feedback	412	3.39	1.273
OL11.c Use digital tools to create online assessment measures	412	3.70	1.141
OL11.d Prepare instructions describing online assessments	414	3.88	1.11
OL11.e Prepare feedback strategies for online setting	413	3.87	1.137

112 ▪ Instructor Competencies

TABLE 7.13 Competencies Related to Learner Engagement

Competency performance statements	N	M	SD
Core 12 Learner Engagement	427	4.00	1
OL12.a Use technologies and tools to engage and motivate online learners	428	4.07	1.025
OL12.b Use technologies and tools to assist in bringing online activities to closure	428	3.93	1.067

cameras) so that learners are engaged, motivated, and able to interact with the content, peers, and the instructor. In addition to considering how to facilitate learner engagement, online instructors will also need to select appropriate tools to facilitate final assessments, synthesis and summary, and critique activities that bring closure. Table 7.13 includes performance statements and descriptive statistics.

13. Instructional Adaptation to Learners/Learning Environment

Learning environments influence learners' experiences and require an instructor to adapt accordingly. In online learning settings, an online instructor can access learner interactions and activities to monitor group dynamic interactions and processes. Through the use of online monitoring features (e.g., access analytics, discussion boards, etc.), instructors can identify who is or is not participating as well as monitor the quality and the nature of the interactions. An online instructor may need to employ online tools to adjust group dynamics for a variety of reasons, including, for example, refocusing learners who are confused or off track or providing additional resources to clarify or enrich understanding. Table 7.14 includes performance statements and descriptive statistics.

14. Learning Promotion Through Feedback

Online feedback can be provided to learners via numerous tools, and online learners often need to be introduced to and instructed on how to provide feedback online. Online instructors are expected to describe and

TABLE 7.14 Competencies Related to Instruction Adaptation to Learners/Learning Environment

Competency performance statements	N	M	SD
Core 13 Instruction Adaptation to Learners/Learning Environment	425	3.77	1.08
OL13.a Monitor online group dynamics	427	3.74	1.118
OL13.b Adjust the use of online tools based on group dynamics	426	3.80	1.153

TABLE 7.15 Competencies Related to Learning Promotion Through Feedback

Competency performance statements	N	M	SD
Core 14 Learning Promotion through Feedback	422	3.79	1.03
OL14.a Instruct learners on feedback mechanisms in online contexts	424	3.83	1.052
OL14.b Enable learners to provide peer feedback using online tools and strategies	426	3.69	1.147
OL14.c Provide learners with feedback using online tools and strategies	424	3.83	1.132

demonstrate online feedback options, but also need to provide instruction for learners on how and when to use the feedback in a variety of formats (e.g., text-based, verbal, video, etc.). Additionally, learners will use different online tools to provide feedback, and an online instructor must allow for opportunities for students to give feedback using digital tools (e.g., apps, surveys, social media, etc.) and while using multiple types of technology (e.g., smart phones, tablets, PCs, etc.). Conversely, an instructor needs these same types of skills to provide learners with necessary, timely, and appropriate feedback. Table 7.15 includes performance statements and descriptive statistics.

15. Retention and Promotion of KSAs

In order to engage online learners throughout all instructional cycles, an online instructor will plan for the use of online tools to promote learner attainment of knowledge, skills, and attitudes. Instructors need to selectively assign digital tools (e.g., collaborative sites such as Google, digital artifacts/images, etc.) to encourage learners to express thinking, revising, rethinking, synthesizing, reflecting and so on. Learners can express thinking through online discussions, share drafts and revise using file sharing services, rethink and synthesize with online concept maps, and reflect with online journals and self-critiques. Table 7.16 includes performance statements and descriptive statistics.

TABLE 7.16 Competencies Related to Retention and Promotion of Knowledge, Skills, and Attitudes

Competency performance statements	N	M	SD
Core 15 Retention and Promotion of KSAs	420	3.98	1.07
OL15.a Engage learners in expressing knowledge, skills, and attitudes in online and offline contexts	420	3.98	1.072

16. Transfer of Learned KSAS to Other Contexts

Instruction is intended to promote and transfer learning to other contexts. The use of many different learning media that include text, imagery, and sound enhances retention, and it is incumbent upon online instructors to use a wide variety of technologies and strategies in order to facilitate learning transfer and application beyond the classroom. A variety of digital tools are available to encourage learners to explore and demonstrate applications outside of instructional examples and to explore applications in other contexts. It is feasible, for example, for learners to create and share infographics with an audience beyond the instructional setting. Table 7.17 includes performance statements and descriptive statistics.

17. Application of Class Management Principles

In online learning environments, instructors must be intentional and explicit when it comes to instructional management. How learners are to participate, use technology, engage in learning, and so on must be clearly delineated using online tools and strategies. Time management is an ongoing issue for online learners, and an instructor needs to engage learners in time management and learning expectations through the use of evidence-based strategies including, for example, learning contracts, discussion policies, virtual notifications, and rubrics. Online instructors can use emails, join in online discussion postings, post announcements, or any other of the multiple ways to communicate online individually or collectively with learners. Should online conflict arise, an online instructor is expected to effectively and efficiently use tools and technologies to mediate and resolve all conflicts. Table 7.18 includes performance statements and descriptive statistics.

TABLE 7.17 Competencies Related to Transfer of Learned KSAs to Other Contexts

Competency performance statements	N	M	SD
Core 16 Transfer of Learned KSAs to Other Contexts	419	4.09	0.99
OL16.a Stimulate application of learning beyond instructional context using online tools and strategies	419	4.09	0.991

TABLE 7.18 Competencies Related to Application of Class Management Principles

Competency performance statements	N	M	SD
Core 17 Application of Class Management Principles	415	3.78	1.14
OL17.a Use online tools and strategies to manage learner behavior	415	3.78	1.14
OL17.b Use tools and strategies to support conflict resolution in the online and offline classroom	425	3.85	1.12

Evaluating Learning

18. Plan and Preparation for Monitoring and Evaluating Instruction

In addition to issues relating to learner privacy, confidentiality, and security, online instructors must also be competent in protecting the evaluation of online courses/materials and instruction. An online instructor may or may not be involved in selecting evaluation criteria, but they often determine who has access rights to the evaluation results. Online instructors are expected to provide online learners with the evaluation context, the benefits/value of evaluating instruction, and clear directions on how to respond to online evaluations. Table 7.19 includes performance statements and descriptive statistics.

19. Evaluation of Instructional Effectiveness

Online instructors are expected to grow and advance; online evaluation findings provide a means to do so. By compiling and analyzing results of measures of quality and effectiveness of instructional strategies, online instructors can devise a basis for improvement. Issues such as the effectiveness of synchronous or asynchronous environments are germane to online instructional impact. Table 7.20 includes performance statements and descriptive statistics.

TABLE 7.19 Competencies Related to Plan and Preparation for Monitoring and Evaluating Instruction

Competency performance statements	N	M	SD
Core 18 Plan and Preparation for Monitoring and Evaluating Instruction	415	3.74	1.04
OL18.a Determine access rights to online evaluation results	418	3.59	1.193
OL18.b Prepare directions for online evaluation activities	418	3.89	1.056

TABLE 7.20 Competencies Related to Evaluation of Instructional Effectiveness

Competency performance statements	N	M	SD
Core 19 Evaluation of Instructional Effectiveness	419	3.97	1.04
OL19.a Compile and analyze evaluation findings from online settings	419	3.97	1.042

STATISTICAL DEMOGRAPHIC DIFFERENCES

In addition to the descriptive statistics reported for the competencies and performance statements, statistical analyses were conducted to analyze instructor differences in their perception of how critical online teaching competencies are based on gender, age, geographic location, highest degree earned, and teaching experience.

Differences Based on Gender

Among the instructors who reported their gender, there were 162 instructors who identified as male, and 190 instructors who identified as female. Among the 19 competencies, male and female instructors significantly differed in their perception of 18 competencies at the $p < .05$ level. There was only one competency where there was no difference in instructor perception based on gender (Competency 2: improvement of instructor practices). Though not significantly different, the female instructors had consistently higher ratings on how critical the competencies were compared to the male instructors on all 19 items.

Previous research on gender and online teaching competencies had mixed findings. Several researchers (Horvitz et al., 2015; Martin, Budhrani, & Wang, 2019; Vang et al., 2020) found specific differences for online teaching, whereas Aydin (2005) found no difference in faculty perception of competencies based on gender. The findings of the current study were aligned to Horvitz et al. (2015), Martin, Budhrani, and Wang (2019), and Vang et al. (2020). Horvitz et al. (2015) found that female faculty reported higher self-efficacy in employing online instruction strategies than male faculty. Vang et al. (2020) also found female faculty perceptions to be significantly higher for course design and course communication in online teaching. Similarly, Martin, Budhrani, and Wang (2019) found female faculty perceptions were significantly higher than male faculty attitudes about the importance of course design, course communication, and time management. In this competency validation study, female faculty had higher perception on 18 out of the 19 competencies.

Differences Based on Age

Among the instructors who provided their age, there were 76 instructors in the 20 to 39 years age range, 105 instructors between 40 to 49 years, 139 instructors between 50 to 59 years, and 85 instructors above 60 years.

Among the 19 competencies, based on their ages, instructors significantly differed in their perception on seven competencies at the $p < .05$ level.

Analysis of variance showed that there were differences in respondent perception on five competencies: 3, 7, 8, 11, and 14. However, post-hoc analysis showed differences only between three competencies for one age range each.

For Competency 3 (anticipation of situational factors) there were differences in respondents between age range 20 to 39, and 50 to 59. The younger range rated this competency as more critical ($M = 4.13$), compared those who were in the 50 to 59 age range ($M = 3.78$).

The other two were Competency 11 (preparation of assessment and feedback) and 14 (learning promotion through feedback), where there were differences between age range 40 to 49, and 50 to 59. In both cases, those in the age range 40 to 49 rated the competency as less critical than those in the age range 50 to 59.

This competency validation study found significant differences based on instructor age in three competencies. This is different from prior research (Mirke & Tzivian, 2021; Sultan et al., 2021), where age did not have any impact on faculty perception of online teaching competencies. Sultan et al. (2021) studied faculty satisfaction for teaching online and found that age did not have any impact. Similarly, Mirke and Tzivian (2021) observed no difference in online teaching readiness between older and younger teachers working at primary, secondary, or vocational educational institutions in Latvia.

Differences Based on Geographic Location

Among the instructors who provided their geographic location, 288 instructors were located in the United States or Canada, and 118 instructors were outside of the United States and Canada. Among the 19 competencies, based on geographic location, instructors significantly differed in their perception on 10 competencies at the $p < .05$ level. These competencies include:

- Competency 2: improvement of instructor practices
- Competency 7: specification of expected learning
- Competency 8: plan of instructional approach
- Competency 9: plan of instructional resources
- Competency 11: preparation of assessment and feedback
- Competency 12: learner engagement
- Competency 14: learning promotion through feedback
- Competency 15: retention and promotion of KSAs

- Competency 18: plan and preparation for monitoring and evaluating instruction
- Competency 19: evaluation of instructional effectiveness

Instructors who were located outside of the United States and Canada rated each of these 10 competencies as more critical than those instructors within the United States and Canada.

Due to the lack of variability among respondents from different countries, they were grouped into the United States or Canada and the rest of the world. There is a need for additional research to collect data globally and analyze the differences among instructors from various parts of the world.

Differences Based on Highest Degree Earned

Among the participants who provided their highest degree earned, 122 instructors had earned a doctoral degree, 144 instructors had earned a master's degree, 61 instructors had earned an undergraduate 2- or 4-year degree, and 79 instructors had earned other degrees. The only significant difference based on instructors' highest degree was for Competency 18: plan and preparation for monitoring and evaluating instruction.

Tukey post-hoc tests showed that for Competency 18, there were differences between respondents with doctoral and master's degree, and between master's and 2- or 4-year undergraduate degrees. The respondents with the master's degree rated this the lowest, while those with doctoral degree rated it the highest, and those with the undergraduate degrees scored in between. This is another variable where we need additional research to examine instructor differences.

Differences Based on Online Teaching Experience

Among the instructors who provided their online teaching experience, 31 instructors had no years of experience, 131 instructors had less than 5 years of experience, 83 instructors had 5 to 10 years of experience, and 104 instructors had more than 10 years of experience. Among the 19 competencies, there were significant differences based on instructor years of online teaching experience on five competencies. These include:

- Competency 1: effective communication, for which there was a significant difference in respondents who had no experience and more than 10 years of experience.

- Competency 12: learner engagement, for which there was a significant difference in respondents who had no experience and those with 5 to 10 years of experience, and more than 10 years of experience.
- Competency 13: instruction adaptation to learners/learning environment, for which there was a significant difference in respondents who had no experience and those with 5 to 10 years of experience, and more than 10 years of experience.
- Competency 15: retention and promotion of KSAs, for which there was a significant difference in respondents who had no experience and those with 5 to 10 years of experience, and more than 10 years of experience. There was also a difference in respondents who had taught less than 5 years and who had taught more than 10 years.
- Competency 17: application of class management principles, for which there was a significant difference in respondents who had no experience and those with less than 5 years, 5 to 10 years of experience, and more than 10 years of experience.

In all these comparisons for which differences were found, those with more years of experience rated the competency as more critical. The findings regarding teaching experience are aligned with research that has shown a positive relationship between faculty years of experience and online teaching. Research has, however, examined self-efficacy rather than how critical these competencies are to online teaching. Shea (2007) found that with more experience, faculty self-confidence increased. Martin, Budhrani, and Wang (2019), when examining faculty members' years of online teaching experience and their attitude towards online teaching, did not find any significant difference. However, when examining faculty members' years of online teaching experience and perception of ability to teach online, Martin, Budhrani, and Wang (2019) found significant differences. Also, Martin, Wang, Jokiaho, May, and Grübmeyer (2019), when comparing competencies between U.S. and German online instructors, found that teaching experience was positively related to self-efficacy, specifically for course design, course communication, and technology.

SUMMARY

This chapter provided the descriptive statistics of competencies and performance statements that instructors consider critical for online teaching, along with explanations describing how the performance statements reflect online instruction and delivery. In addition, we discussed the differences based on instructor demographic characteristics (gender, age, geographic location, highest degree earned, and online teaching experience) for online instruction. Significant differences are also reported in the respondents' perceptions of how critical the competencies for online instruction are based on gender, age, geographic location, highest degree earned, and online teaching experience.

REFERENCES

Aydin, C. H. (2005). Turkish mentors' perception of roles, competencies and resources for online teaching. *Turkish Online Journal of Distance Education, 6*(3), 1–23. https://dergipark.org.tr/en/pub/tojde/issue/16929/176725

Horvitz, B. S., Beach, A. L., Anderson, M. L., & Xia, J. (2015). Examination of faculty self-efficacy related to online teaching. *Innovative Higher Education, 40*(4), 305–316. http://doi.org/10.1007/s10755-014-9316-1

Martin, F., Budhrani, K., & Wang, C. (2019). Examining faculty perception of their readiness to teach online. *Online Learning Journal, 23*(3), 97–119. http://doi.org/10.24059/olj.v23i3.1555

Martin, F., Wang, C., Jokiaho, A., May, B., & Grübmeyer, S. (2019). Examining faculty readiness to teach online: A comparison of US and German educators. *European Journal of Open, Distance and E-learning, 22*(1), 53–69. http://doi.org/10.2478/eurodl-2019-0004

Mathes, J. (2020). *A defining moment for online learning.* Online Learning Consortium Blog. https://onlinelearningconsortium.org/a-defining-moment-for-online-learning

Mirke, E., & Tzivian, L. (2021, April). Teachers' readiness for remote teaching during COVID-19 pandemic: The case of Latvia. In *2021 IEEE Global Engineering Education Conference (EDUCON)* (pp. 537–542). IEEE. https://doi.org/10.1109/EDUCON46332.2021.9454088

Shea, P. (2007). Bridges and barriers to teaching online college courses: A study of experienced faculty in thirty-six colleges. *Journal of Asynchronous Learning Networks, 11*(2), 73–128. http://doi.org/10.24059/olj.v11i2.1728

Sultan, R. A., Alqallaf, A. K., Alzarooni, S. A., Alrahma, N. H., AlAli, M. A., & Alshurideh, M. T. (2021, June). How students influence faculty satisfaction with online courses and do the age of faculty matter [Conference paper]. In *The International Conference on Artificial Intelligence and Computer Vision* (pp. 823–837). Springer. https://doi.org/10.1007/978-3-030-76346-6_72

Vang, K., Martin, F., & Wang, C. (2020). Examining community college faculty perceptions of their preparedness to teach online. *Journal of Applied Research in the Community College, 27*(1), 45–63. https://www.researchgate.net/publication/340949801

CHAPTER 8

INSTRUCTOR COMPETENCIES

Growth-Mindset Orientation and Continuous Development

CHAPTER OVERVIEW

The IBSTPI competencies definition, as described in the first chapter of this book, was slightly modified during the current revision of the IBSTPI instructor competencies. The modification to the definition focuses on the inclusion of "a growth identity" characteristic and is explained in detail in this chapter. More specifically, this chapter describes why an instructor's growth-mindset orientation is integral to an instructor's overall competence, along with a discussion of existing literature supporting mindset. This chapter also discusses instructor competency sets that are beginning to include growth mindsets, as well as how the rapid infusion of technology in our instructional settings clearly illustrates that competent instructors need to have a growth-mindset disposition that allows for perceiving failures as opportunities. Finally, the chapter concludes with recommendations for instructors to engage in continuous development.

122 • Instructor Competencies

> **Orienting Questions**
> - Why is a growth-mindset orientation an expectation for today's instructors?
> - How can we support instructors' growth mindsets and continuous development?

DEVELOPMENTAL GROWTH AND INSTRUCTOR COMPETENCIES

Today's dynamic instructional settings place many demands on instructors as they strive to implement instructional advances described in empirical findings on teaching and learning and as they experiment with a broad range and scope of emerging tools and technologies. Within such complex settings, which are often hampered by workplace constraints, instructors are expected to gain, maintain, or improve their knowledge, skills, and attitudes (KSAs) and demonstrate competence in their field. Developmental growth is an ongoing process as instructors are expected to become increasingly adaptive to instructional practice and environments. Models of pre-service teachers' stages of development predominantly have displayed growth as hierarchical and linear; however, Khoshnevisan and Rashtchi (2021) offers a five-stage model that illustrates the nonlinear and multilayer stages of developmental growth, and it highlights how experience, knowledge, and practice lead to increases in pre-service instructors' competence. In considering developmental growth and instructional competence, one must note that this developmental model "asserts that there is no ending to the professional development of teachers, and it is a never-ending process" (Khoshnevisan & Rashtchi, 2021, p. 16). In any developmental growth stage that an instructor experiences, those who possess a growth-mindset orientation are the ones who will seek professional development. According to Dweck (2016), these individuals are more likely to achieve more because looking smart isn't what drives them; instead, they put their energy into learning.

How an instructor perceives their own potential and capabilities influences many aspects of their instructional persona and practices. Any instructor who adopts a fixed mindset (Dweck, 2008) based on the belief that intellectual ability is a dispositional attribute, perceives mistakes as failures. There are other instructors, however, who adopt a growth mindset (Dweck, 2008) based on the belief that intellectual skills and abilities are incrementally acquired through hard work and perseverance. In fact, these individuals may learn more, learn more quickly, and view challenges and failures as opportunities to improve their learning and skills. People may also have a mindset related to their personal or professional lives—"I'm a good teacher" or "I'm a bad parent," for example.

People can be aware or unaware of their mindsets, but according to Dweck (2016), mindsets can have profound effects on learning achievement, skill acquisition, personal relationships, professional success, and many other dimensions of life. It is those instructors with a growth mindset that seek possibilities for developmental growth in their professional practice through training, education, and mentored experiences. Stagnation of developmental growth can become an occupational hazard in today's dynamic instructional settings. Therefore, an emphasis on cultivating growth-mindset approaches is recognized as essential to performing an instructor's job properly. The IBSTPI competency definition now includes this powerful concept:

> A set of related knowledge, skills, attitudes and *a growth identity* that enable an individual to effectively perform the activities of a given occupation or job function to the standards expected in employment.

Regardless of job roles and domains of practice, instructors' perceived need for developmental growth is largely shaped by a professional identity that values high standards of performance and lifelong development. Developing professional identity also needs to include a broad perspective and the importance of "teacher as learner" and "teacher as professional" (Bolton, 2010) and to be largely driven by a growth identity shaping one's vision of higher levels of effectiveness in practice throughout the lifespan (Argyris & Schön, 1974; Burke & Stets, 2009). Yet, according to Boyd (2014), "One paradox of the academic profession is that we get so busy teaching that we prevent ourselves from engaging in deep learning situations" (p. 30). It is a vision of future growth, however, that drives intrinsic motivation for addressing complicated or complex challenges increasingly encountered over time in professional practice (Dweck, 2016). An instructor who possesses a growth mindset can be self-motivated to stretch their competencies limits so that they can accomplish difficult and worthwhile tasks across a variety of challenges encountered in practice. In our increasingly complex world, professionals with a growth mindset are increasingly aware that continuous learning is a must. Relative to a growth mindset are an instructor's epistemological beliefs (EB), that is, beliefs on the nature of knowledge, how knowledge is acquired, and ways of knowing. In the research literature there are varying definitions and views of what constitutes EB. These perspectives are viewed as "contrasts between transmission of knowledge vs construction of knowledge and various stances toward knowledge such as acceptance, puzzlement, or doubt" (Hanson, 2020, p. 31). Furthermore, an instructor's beliefs about intelligence do more than influence their own behaviors and interactions; these beliefs also influence learner perceptions of intellectual abilities and capabilities of perseverance.

It is recognized that in any classroom or workplace setting, the perceptions of powerful people such as instructors or employers shape the goals and behavior of others (Murphy & Dweck, 2010). Murphy and Dweck report that in a given context, a decision maker's verbal and nonverbal behavior, reward structures, and/or evaluation policies can endorse either a fixed or growth mindset. Instructors' implicit theories of intelligence influence instructional practice through instructional methods and language usage. A study by Gwathney (2021) queried instructors at private and public community colleges and four-year institutions to assess their implicit theories of intelligence. The findings indicate that faculty generally think their students possess a growth mindset, but these students may also possess fixed mindsets. While the body of evidence is still small, faculty members' implicit theories are more impactful than their gender, race, ethnicity, or tenure status, as predictors of their students' achievement and motivation (Canning et al., 2019). In higher education, for example, there are empirical findings related to the impact of faculty who endorse growth versus fixed mindsets. Fuesting et al. (2019) looked across eight studies highlighting how instructors' mindsets communicated to students in STEM courses whether or not students had the ability to succeed and whether or not they would want to succeed. These findings suggest that faculty mindset behaviors do have implications when it comes to learners seeking help and providing it to others. Instructor mindset behaviors were also found to influence learner understanding of whether or not an academic pathway might be worth pursuing.

For the most part, growth-mindset studies have been conducted at all levels of educational settings, but research is ongoing in other organizations to study for example, leadership (Dennis, 2016), mentoring (Stelter et al., 2020), and creativity (Zhou et al., 2020). Based on the effects of growth mindset cited in human resource development literature, Han and Stieha (2020) advocate for growth-mindset interventions in three primary areas: career development, training and development, and organizational development.

A body of evidence exists to support that a growth mindset empowers learners' performance and academic engagement, enabling them to persist when facing challenges and difficulties; however, there is a need to empirically study important issues such as "how teachers' mindsets influence their work engagement, well-being, and perseverance in the educational settings" (Zeng et al., 2019, p. 839). The concept of work engagement, simply described as an employee's level of dedication and enthusiasm towards their work, is a related aspect to an instructor's growth or fixed mindset. According to Schaufeli and Salanova (2011), work engagement can be a "slippery term," but an operational definition needs to include the core dimensions of vigor, which produces high levels of energy, and mental resilience and dedication, which result in active engagement with a sense of significance, enthusiasm, and challenge. Instruction and our understanding of it is dynamic, and instructors must be adaptable and willing to learn. We must also continue to study whether belief-based interventions for instructors can promote increases in growth mindsets; more studies are needed like Seaton's (2018) research on the positive influence on teachers receiving mindset training enabling their ability to implement adaptive motivation instruction, and the study conducted by Irie et al. (2018) indicating it may be necessary for teacher education programs to explicitly develop interpersonal skills, since their data found preservice teachers believe in the learnability of instructional technical skills but regard interpersonal skills as an individual fixed talent.

We recognize that in today's instructional workplaces there are many demands placed on instructors, challenging their mental resilience and possibly resulting in doubts about their own abilities to meet the challenges. In the face of such challenges, instructors are very likely to discern gaps with existing levels of competence and may lack the energy or means to address novel or complex instructional problems. As a thought exercise, consider how the IBSTPI key foundational competencies can come into play when an instructor is faced with making sense of novel or complex situational factors that require advanced levels of cognitive reasoning. Instructors need insight to support creative design but also may require deeper levels of ethical reasoning if solutions are likely to diverge from existing standards of practice. Creative thought involved with insight is associated with the means to look at challenges from different angles and synthesize disparate perspectives into new revelations or approaches (Csikszentmihalyi, 1999). For example, creativity in the use of instructional competencies allows for an openness in looking at instructional design options through the use of diverse perspectives. This openness allows for instructional competencies to be applied in novel ways that are better able to address new or complex challenges. Additionally, instructors are guiding learners through increasingly complex learning that requires "integrating knowledge, skills and abilities; coordinating qualitatively different constituent skills, and often transferring what is learned in the school or training setting to daily life and work settings" (Kirschner & van Merriënboer, 2013, p. 244).

Reflective thinking is considered a higher-level thinking skill, and instructors perform this reflection at three levels: technical, practical, and critical (van Manen, 1977). It is at the highest level of reflection, that is at the critical level that encompasses both technical and practical reflection, where instructors are "approached with a critical point of view during and after the actions" (Orakci, 2021, p. 119). Orakci (2021) continues: "While making critical reflection, the individual uses not only the knowledge he/

she has but also the infrastructure that constitutes it (sociocultural environment, religion, language, family structure, tradition, customs, etc.)" (p. 119).

Reflective practice is an essential process in an instructor's development, and accordingly, "Teachers can confidently expect to raise their standards of professional confidence through adopting processes of reflective teaching" (Bera & Mohalik, 2015, p. 177). The need to be a reflective practitioner is called for in a variety of instructional settings. As an example, the National Standards for Quality (NSQ, n.d.) that provides K–12 online and blended communities include in their standard on professional responsibilities that an online/blended teacher is a reflective practitioner. Higher levels of professional effectiveness with instructor competencies, while semi-independent, can be increasingly fused and applied in reflective practice calling for ideological commitments beyond self-interest. As cognitive and ethical reasoning becomes increasingly mature in professional practice, there is greater wisdom or discernment about why and how best to employ competencies to better address complex learning and instructional challenges benefiting from shared effort. The means to apply cognitive and ethical reasoning well in collaboration for problem solving in the profession is key to effectiveness with novel or complex challenges (Argyris & Schön, 1974).

SUPPORTING INSTRUCTORS' GROWTH MINDSET

IBSTPI's competency definition now includes a "growth mindset," as stated above and the inclusion of this powerful concept in studies or application of instructor competency sets is underway. For example, Graham et al. (2022) developed K–12 blended teaching competencies that include a growth orientation because, "Becoming a successful blended teacher will require you to take risks. You may fail at times, but these failures can help you learn and improve" (Graham et al., 2022, p. 14). Through the use of identity theory and research, Stricker et al. (2019) have introduced a professional identity development framework along the dimensions of cognitive and moral reasoning. In its early stages of development, this framework uses the profession of arms to illustrate how it can serve as a guide for developmental instruction to engage higher levels of growth and maturation in professionals. The key constructs for military "guardian" identity include the "Doing Self," who is virtuous and possesses moral and ethical courage; the "Thinking Self," who is intelligent and wise; and the "Making Self," who possess a growth mindset (Stricker et al., 2019). The profession of arms includes a broad range of expertise, and this identity developmental framework has application across all professionals and is applicable to an instructor's growth. Developing a professional identity as an instructor is a sense-making process that leads to developing an image of self as a teacher (Cobb, 2020).

While the concept of mindsets applies to everyone and across different contexts, a current area of interest is how to develop a growth mindset in instructors. If we look to the K–12 arena, the website Edutopia promotes developing a growth mindset in teachers through these professional development strategies: modeling a growth mindset to encourage teachers to see themselves as learners; creating space for new ideas to encourage a willingness to try new approaches; building time for self-reflection to consider what was learned from a process and not its success or failure; and including formative performance feedback that promotes instructor participation in the feedback process (Heggart, 2015). When instructors don't possess the belief that intellectual abilities can be developed, instructors can receive a growth-mindset intervention. Although psychological interventions can be effective in changing the ways that people do sense making, Yeager et al. (2022) are exploring where a growth-mindset intervention works and where it does not. In a paper using data from the National Study of Learning Mindsets, the researchers studied whether teachers' mindset beliefs or the practices that follow from them do play a direct, causal role in student learning. They found that more experimental research is needed to identify where a growth mindset works best.

While a growth mindset is expected of today's instructors, a digital mindset is also becoming an expectation. Initially, instructors needed to develop digital literacy, "the ability to properly use and evaluate digital resources, tools, and services, and apply it to lifelong learning processes" (Gilster, 1997, p. 220). In the ensuing years, digital technologies have become more user-friendly and prevalent in many settings. Thus, it has become apparent that a skills-focused digital literacy approach is too limited. An instructor today must possess teacher digital competence (TDC). With digital competence comes "the knowledge, capacities and attitudes of using digital technologies to consume, evaluate, and create learning information and to collaborate and communicate with others for learning information and to collaborate and communicate with others for learning purposes" (Janssen et al., 2013, p. 482). The need for digital competence goes beyond instructors and is expected of students and citizens. The European Union (2018) established digital competence as a key competency for lifelong learning, and yet, as Janssen et al. (2013) assert, how one demonstrates digital competency lacks clarity and practical terms. Similarly, the International Society for Technology in Education (ISTE) recommends that educators should be learners as they continually improve their practice by learning. Specifically, in ISTE standards for educators, 2.1a states the importance of setting professional learning goals, 2.1b states the importance of pursuing professional interests, and 2.1c states the importance of staying current with research

(ISTE, 2023a). The promotion of ongoing development is also reflected in standard 3.5 for educational leaders, who are to be connected learners who "model and promote continuous professional learning for themselves and others" (ISTE, 2023b).

The notion of teacher digital competence is also reflected in the foundational work of the TPACK framework (technological pedagogical content knowledge) to describe the types of knowledge teachers need in contemporary diverse classroom settings (Mishra & Koehler, 2006). The TPACK framework suggests that effective teachers should possess technological knowledge, pedagogical knowledge, and content knowledge in 21st century classrooms. These different types of knowledge intersect to form more complex forms of knowledge (such as pedagogical content knowledge) that represent the basis of good teaching with technology and require the following:

> An understanding of the representation of concepts using technologies; pedagogical techniques that use technologies in constructive ways to teach content; knowledge of what makes concepts difficult or easy to learn and how technology can help redress some of the problems that students face; knowledge of students' prior knowledge and theories of epistemology; and knowledge of how technologies can be used to build on existing knowledge and to develop new epistemologies or strengthen old ones. (Mishra & Koehler, 2006, p. 1029)

The TPACK framework has been used to measure pre-service teacher knowledge (Ritzhaupt et al., 2016), develop professional development experiences for teachers (Koh et al., 2017), and frame the nature of pre-service teacher education programs (Jang & Chen, 2010).

Empirical evidence as to what constitutes instructors' digital competence is an emerging field of study in teacher education. The need to prepare future teachers to effectively use digital technologies is not new, but the prior limited focus on technology skills is no longer sufficient; instead, a more holistic, integrated approach is a path forward. While there is no consensus on the best methods to develop pre-service teacher digital competence, recent studies suggest that broader considerations around using technology and its impact be included. Falloon presents a scoping review of existing frameworks guiding teacher digital development and indicates insufficiencies given that they do not address "the present skills-focused digital literacy emphasis be abandoned, in favour of broader digital competency models that recognise the more diverse knowledge, capabilities and dispositions needed by future teachers" (Falloon, 2020, p. 2451.) A significant contribution of Falloon's paper is the introduction of the TDC framework that integrates three fundamental competencies: curriculum-related, personal-ethical, and personal-professional. It is the third pillar, providing a dispositional and functional competency, that needs to be highlighted here because of its advocacy of a positive mindset needed to engage in continuous learning. An instructor needs to engage in ongoing learning and adaptations when it comes to technology integration. Due to the rapid changes with digital technologies, instructors are expected to monitor and enhance their own digital skills. Martin et al. (2021) identified "lifelong learner" to be one of the roles of the online instructor. This role included competencies such as integrating research-based best practices, participating in professional development, sharing, and learning from colleagues, continuously improving the courses based on data, and keeping up with the advancement in educational technologies.

RECOMMENDATIONS FOR INSTRUCTORS' CONTINUOUS DEVELOPMENT

Professional development (PD) for instructors is helpful to continuously develop knowledge, skills, and abilities needed to have the foundational, design, facilitation, and evaluation competencies discussed in the current book. Dysart and Weckerle (2015) present a conceptual model for practice-based professional development to include learning by design during the training, peer coaching during teaching, and communities of practice beyond training. In a study when teachers were asked about their professional development needs in Turkey, Bayar (2014) found that teachers indicated that PD should match their needs, match the needs of their school, provide opportunity for them to be involved in the design of the PD, provide room for active participation and longer-term engagement, and have high-quality instructors. In another study examining the needs of college faculty, Wynants and Dennis (2018) found that control of pace, flexibility, and continued access to resources were important aspects of professional development. These are all critical elements for effective professional development that supports instructors' continuous development, along with recognition that engaging in professional development is essential for instructors' growth. For example, AdvanceHE's professional standards framework includes as a core activity instructor enhancement through continuing professional development (AdvanceHE, 2020).

Instructors can also benefit from dedicated time set aside to work towards their professional growth. Centers for faculty development and professional organizations focusing on teaching and learning offer workshops and presentations on best practices in teaching for instructors to continue to develop the competencies and keep up with up-to-date knowledge and skills. Administrators at various organizations are recommended to provide opportunities for continuous development for instructors and also opportunities for peer engagement through which instructors learn from and share with each other. Stewart (2014) discusses the benefits for instructors who are a part of a professional learning community. Instructors who have content expertise in various subjects are also encouraged to review research on teaching and learning and integrate best practices and strategies into their content-based courses. For example, Neck and Corbett (2018) discuss scholarship of teaching and learning in entrepreneurship.

With technology advancement and COVID-19 enforcing digital learning, more instructors are expected to have competencies to teach through different delivery modalities including hybrid, online, Hyflex, and so on. Baran and Correia (2014) offer a three-level professional development framework for online learning, with organization-level support focusing on rewards, recognition, and organizational culture. Community-level support includes learning groups, peer support, and mentoring programs, while teaching support includes workshops/showcases, training programs, and one-on-one assistance. In another study examining professional development needs, Martin et al. (2019) identified aspects of administrative support for online instructors, including more time to prepare courses; inclusion of course development as part of teaching load; smaller class sizes; and recognizing quality of courses (Martin et al., 2019). Utilizing the various recommendations and strategies discussed in this section, instructors can work towards continually developing themselves with the competencies they require to excel in their teaching.

CONCLUSION

This chapter described how instructors' growth-mindset orientation is integral to an instructor's overall competence. It also discussed the instructor competencies that are beginning to include growth mindsets and continuous development, and how technology advancement in instructional practices illustrates a growth-mindset disposition. Finally, the chapter includes recommendations for instructors to engage in continuous development.

REFERENCES

AdvanceHE. (n.d.). *Helping HE shape its future.* Retrieved March 17, 2023, from https://advance-he.ac.uk/about-us

Argyris, C., & Schön, D. A. (1974). *Theory in practice: Increasing professional effectiveness.* Jossey-Bass.

Baran, E., & Correia, A. P. (2014). A professional development framework for online teaching. *TechTrends, 58*(5), 95–101. https://doi.org/10.1007/s11528-014-0791-0

Bayar, A. (2014). The components of effective professional development activities in terms of teachers' perspective. *International Online Journal of Educational Sciences, 6*(2), 319–327. https://files.eric.ed.gov/fulltext/ED552871.pdf

Bera, S., & Mohalik, R. (2015). Reflective practice in professional development of teachers. In N. Mitra (Ed.), *Prospects and challenges of teacher education in India* (p. 177–186). Siliguri B. Ed College. https://www.researchgate.net/publication/349212289

Bolton, G. (2010). *Reflective practice: Writing & professional development* (3rd ed.). SAGE.

Boyd, D. (2014). The growth mindset approach: A threshold concept in course redesign. *Journal on Centers for Teaching and Learning, 6*, 29–44. https://openjournal.lib.miamioh.edu/index.php/jctl/article/view/139

Burke, P. J., & Stets, J. E. (2009). *Identity theory.* Oxford University Press.

Canning, E., Muenks, K., Green, D., & Murphy, M. (2019). STEM faculty who believe ability is fixed have larger racial achievement gaps and inspire less student motivation in their classes. *Science Advances, 5*(2), 1–7. https://doi.org/10.1126/sciadv.aau4734

Cobb, D. J. (2020). Initial teacher education and the development of teacher identity. In M. A. Peters (Ed.), *Encyclopedia of teacher education* (pp. 1–5). Springer. https://doi.org/10.1007/978-981-13-1179-6_383-1

Csikszentmihalyi, M. (1999). Implications of a systems perspective for the study of creativity. In Robert J. Sternberg (Ed.), *Handbook of creativity.* Cambridge University Press.

Dennis, K. S. (2016). Cultivating a growth mindset for effective adaptation in today's dynamic workplace. *International Journal on Lifelong Education and Leadership, 2*(2), 1–11. https://dergipark.org.tr/tr/download/article-file/551080

Dweck, C. S. (2008). Can personality be changed? The role of beliefs in personality and change. *Current Directions in Psychological Science, 17*(6), 391–394. https://doi.org/10.1111/j.1467-8721.2008.00612.x

Dweck, C. S. (2016). *Mindset: The new psychology of success* (Updated edition). Ballantine Books.

Dysart, S. A., & Weckerle, C. (2015). Professional development in higher education: A model for meaningful technology integration. *Journal of Information Technology Education. Innovations in Practice, 14*, 255–265. https://doi.org/10.28945/2326

European Union. (2018). Council recommendation of 22 May 2018 on key competences for lifelong learning. *Official Journal of the European Union, 4*, 1–13. https://eur-lex.europa.eu/legal-content/EN/TXT/PDF/?uri=CELEX:32018H0604(01)

Falloon, G. (2020). *Educational Techno*From digital literacy to digital competence: The teacher digital competency (TDC) framework*logy Research and Development, 68*(5), 2449–2472. https://doi.org/10.1007/s11423-020-09767-4

Fuesting, M., Diekman, A., Boucher, K., Murphy, M., Manson, D., & Safer, B. (2019). Growing STEM: Perceived faculty mindset as an indicator of communal affordances in STEM. *Journal of Personality and Social Psychology, 117*(2), 260–281. https://doi.org/10.1037/pspa0000154

Gilster, P. (1997). *Digital literacy.* Wiley.

Graham, C., Borup, J., Jensen, M., Arnesen, K., & Short, C. (2022). *K–12 blended teaching: A guide to practice within the disciplines* (Vol. 2). EdTech Books. https://edtechbooks.org/k12blended2

Gwathney, A. (2021). Resources for higher education faculty: Development of the growth mindset curriculum for college instructors. *PCOM Psychology Dissertations, 562*. https://digitalcommons.pcom.edu/psychology_dissertations/562

Han, S., & Sticha, V. (2020). Growth mindset for human resource development: A scoping review of the literature with recommended interventions. *Human Resource Development Review, 19*(3), 309–331. https://doi.org/10.1177/1534484320939739

Hanson, J. (2020). Testing the relationship between teachers' epistemological beliefs (EB) and a faculty's school growth mindset: Inter-cultural comparison of EB between east and west. *Journal of Organizational Psychology, 20*(4), 31–52. https://doi.org/10.33423/jop.v20i4.3207

Heggart, K. (2015, February 4). *Developing a growth mindset in teachers and staff*. Edutopia. https://www.edutopia.org/discussion/developing-growth-mindset-teachers-and-staff

Irie, K., Ryan, S., & Mercer, S. (2018). Using Q methodology to investigate pre-service EFL teachers' mindset about teaching competences. *Studies in Second Language Learning and Teaching, 8*(3), 575–598. https://doi.org/10.14746/ssllt.2018.8.3.3

ISTE. (2023a). *ISTE standards: Educators*. https://www.iste.org/standards/iste-standards-for-teachers

ISTE. (2023b). *ISTE standards: Education leaders*. https://www.iste.org/standards/iste-standards-for-education-leaders

Jang, S. J., & Chen, K. C. (2010). From PCK to TPACK: Developing a transformative model for pre-service science teachers. *Journal of Science Education and Technology, 19*, 553–564. https://doi.org/10.1007/s10956-010-9222-y

Janssen, J., Stoyanov, S., Ferrari, A., Punie, Y., Pannekeet, K., and Sloep, P. (2013). Experts' views on digital competence: Commonalities and differences. *Computers & Education, 68*, 473–481. https://doi.org/10.1016/j.compedu.2013.06.008

Khoshnevisan, B., & Rashtchi, M. (2021). The first field experience: Perceptions of ESOL pre-service teachers. *Advances in Language and Literary Studies, 12*(5), 15–22. https://files.eric.ed.gov/fulltext/EJ1335616.pdf

Kirschner, P., & van Merriënboer, J. (2013). *Ten steps to complex learning: A new approach to instruction and instructional design*. http://web.mit.edu/xtalks/TenStepsToComplexLearning-Kirschner-VanMerrienboer.pdf

Koh, J. H. L., Chai, C. S., & Lim, W. Y. (2017). Teacher professional development for TPACK-21CL: Effects on teacher ICT integration and student outcomes. *Journal of Educational Computing Research, 55*(2), 172–196.

Martin, F., Kumar, S., & She, L. (2021). Examining higher education instructor roles and competencies for online teaching. *Online Learning, 25*(4), 187–215.

Martin, F., Wang, C., Budhrani, K., Moore, R. L., & Jokiaho, A. (2019). Professional development support for the online instructor: Perspectives of U.S. and German instructors. *Online Journal of Distance Learning Administration, 22*(3). https://eric.ed.gov/?id=EJ1228757

Mishra, P., & Koehler, M. J. (2006). Technological pedagogical content knowledge: A framework for teacher knowledge. *Teachers College Record, 108*(6), 1017–1054. https://doi.org/10.1111/j.1467-9620.2006.00684.x

Murphy, M., & Dweck, C. (2010). A culture of genius: How an organization's lay theory shapes people's cognition, affect, and behavior. *Personality and Social Psychology Bulletin, 36*(3), 283–296. https://doi.org/10.1177/0146167209347380

Neck, H. M., & Corbett, A. C. (2018). The scholarship of teaching and learning entrepreneurship. *Entrepreneurship Education and Pedagogy, 1*(1), 8–41. https://doi.org/10.1177/2515127417737286

Orakci, S. (2021). Teachers' reflection and level of reflective thinking on the different dimensions of their teaching practice. *International Journal of Modern Education Studies, 5*(1), 118–139. https://doi.org/10.51383/ijonmes.2021.88

Ritzhaupt, A. D., Huggins-Manley, A. C., Ruggles, K., & Wilson, M. (2016). Validation of the survey of pre-service teachers' knowledge of teaching and technology: A multi-institutional sample. *Journal of Digital Learning in Teacher Education, 32*(1), 26–37. https://doi.org/10.1080/21532974.2015.1099481

Schaufeli, W., & Salanova, M. (2011). Work engagement: On how to better catch a slippery concept. *European Journal of Work and Organizational Psychology, 20*(1), 39–46. https://doi.org/10.1080/1359432X.2010.515981

Seaton, F. (2018). Empowering teachers to implement a growth mindset. *Educational Psychology in Practice, 34*(1), 41–57. https://doi.org/10.1080/02667363.2017.1382333

Stelter, R., Kupersmidt, J., & Stump, K. (2020). Establishing effective STEM mentoring relationships through mentor training. *Annals of the New York Academy of Sciences, 1483*(1), 224–243. https://doi.org/10.1111/nyas.14470

Stewart, C. (2014). Transforming professional development to professional learning. *Journal of Adult Education, 43*(1), 28–33. https://eric.ed.gov/?id=EJ1047338

Stricker, A., Westhauser, T., Lyle, D., Lowry, C., & Sheets, T. (2019). Identity growth in the professions. In A. G. Stricker, C. Calongne, B. Truman, & F. J. Arenas (Eds.), *Recent advances in applying identity and society awareness to virtual learning* (pp. 27–59). IGI Global.

van Manen, M. (1977). Linking ways of knowing with ways of being practical. *Curriculum Inquiry, 6*(3), 205–228. https://doi.org/10.1080/03626784.1977.11075533

Wynants, S., & Dennis, J. (2018). Professional development in an online context: Opportunities and challenges from the voices of college faculty. *Journal of Educators Online, 15*(1), n1. https://doi.org/10.9743/JEO2018.15.1.2

Yeager, D., Carroll, J., Buontempo, J., Cimpian, A., Woody, S., Crosnoe, R., Muller, C., Murray, J., Mhatre, P., Kersting, N., Hulleman, C., Kudym, M., Murphy, M., Duckworth, A., Walton, G., & Dweck, C. (2022). Teacher mindsets help explain where a growth-mindset intervention does and doesn't work. *Psychological Science, 33*(1), 18–32. https://doi.org/10.1177/09567976211028984

Zeng, G., Xinjie, C., Yan, C., & Kaiping, P. (2019). Teachers' growth mindset and work engagement in Chinese educational context: Well-being and perseverance of effort as mediators. *Frontiers in Psychology, 10*, 1–10. https://doi.org/10.3389/fpsyg.2019.00839

Zhou, Y., Yang, W., & Bai, X. (2020). Creative mindsets: Scale validation in the Chinese setting and generalization to the real workplace. *Frontiers in Psychology, 11*, 463. https://doi.org/10.3389/fpsyg.2020.00463

AFTERWORD

In many respects, the revised set of IBSTPI instructor competencies presented in this book is long overdue. With close to a 20-year gap between these 2021 competencies and the last ones published in 2004, the enterprise of teaching and learning has advanced significantly due to advances in learning sciences, evidence-based pedagogy, emerging technologies, and instructional delivery modalities, but it also remains grounded in well-established instructional principles. The empirical findings from our study conducted to rate the importance of IBSTPI-identified instructor competencies illustrates that many fundamentals of good instruction are holding true, but at the same time, instructors are adapting and enhancing instruction through the use of new understandings on how to instruct using current best practices and how, when appropriate, to effectively integrate digital tools and resources into teaching and learning.

As we write about these revised instructor competencies, a global COVID-19 pandemic dramatically forced educators, instructors, trainers, and learning developers to adapt and re-evaluate instructional methods and delivery platforms and tools. While the empirical study of the IBSTPI instructor competencies conducted in this book precedes the pandemic, the writing of the book occurred during this time of radical shifts and experimentation. What is contained in this book is relevant to those in the teaching and learning field as they navigate our "brave new world." It is germane to note that the 2021 IBSTPI competency definition, as described in the first chapter of this book, was slightly modified during this revision of the instructor competencies. The modification to the definition speaks to a vision of the evolution of instructor competency that includes "a growth identity" characteristic and is explained in detail in Chapter 8. Our modified definition of competency is: "A set of related knowledge, skills, and attitudes, and a growth identity that enable an individual to effectively perform the activities of a given occupation or job function to the standards expected in employment."

Instructors at all levels and in all contexts are called upon to address new and ongoing challenges while adjusting to fast-paced technological advances. In today's world, it is hard to imagine that a growth identity is not a necessary attribute needed to effectively teach and learn.

IBSTPI's historical definitions of competency have traditionally included only knowledge, skills, and attitudes as these concepts can be assessed and observed in the instructor's professional practices to effectively perform their given job roles and functions in the workplace. Previous conceptions of IBSTPI definitions and competencies include the following: the 2006 IBSTPI evaluator competencies, the 2012 IBSTPI instructional designer competencies, the 2012 online learner competencies, and the retired 2004 IBSTPI training manager competencies.

The addition of "a growth identity" is a major leap in the evolution of the IBSTPI competency definition, as the concept itself is a different type of psychological variable—a belief commonly referred to as the growth mindset—which embraces personal characteristics, such as intellectual abilities, that can be developed and enhanced through hard work and persistence, whereas a fixed mindset is the belief that these characteristics are fixed and unchangeable (Yeager & Dweck, 2020). Findings from recent research illustrate that instructors' implicit beliefs reflecting either a growth mindset or fixed mindset orientation moderated their students' learning outcomes in a large, randomized control trial in mathematics classrooms (Yeager et al., 2022). Another study indicated that a growth mindset among instructors was also associated with emotions like enjoyment, which mediated a relationship with work engagement, but only for teachers classified with a growth mindset (Frondozo et al., 2022). While growth mindset research is still a nascent area of inquiry, emerging evidence suggests a growth mindset may be a critical aspect to both learners and instructors.

Many contend that the human brain is designed to struggle and that a growth mindset facilitates human endeavors to be able to learn and grow no matter the setting. IBSTPI's modified definition of competency opens the door to the professional identity formation of an instructor as a framework for professional learning and development. The professional identity of an instructor is a dynamic and ongoing process with different contexts, people, and relationships influencing how instructors conceive of their professional identities and their agency to develop professionally.

In recognition of the significance of instructor professional development, the modified IBSTPI competency definition calls for a reflective instructor capable of growing from different teaching and learning experiences by deeply reflecting on their practice in the instructional setting (Körkkö et al., 2016; Zeichner & Liston, 2013).

While the 2004 IBSTPI instructor competencies and standards incorporated the emerging and evolving roles of face-to-face, online, and blended instructors, the 2021 IBSTPI instructor competencies and standards took these roles a step further by creating separate standards exclusively for core, online, and blended instructional settings that are aligned to the competencies and domains. The current 2021 IBSTPI competencies contain relevant domains pertinent to instructors across instructional settings (i.e., core, blended, and online): (a) professional foundations, (b) designing for learning, (c) facilitating learning, and (d) evaluation of learning. Notably, the 2003 IBSTPI instructor competencies were composed of five domains: (a) professional foundations, (b) planning and preparation, (c) instructional methods and strategies, (d) assessment and evaluation, and (e) management. During the analysis phase of our study, the criticality data, qualitative data, and literature findings guided us as we reviewed the 2004 statements by deciding which ones could be retained, revised, or deleted. As illustrated in Table 9.1, many revisions were made.

The 2021 IBSTPI instructor competencies model revised the domains by reconfiguring the domains based on the research literature on contemporary conceptions of instructors. The 2004 IBSTPI instructor competencies and standards were composed of the five domains, 18 competencies across those domains, and 98 unique performance statements. Seventy-nine core performance statements, 43 blended performance statements, 44 online performance statements, for a total of 166 instructor performance statements across the core, blended, and online instructional configurations. In this new iteration of the competencies, performance statements are provided for each instructional configuration along with separate chapters describing the validation study results for each of the three instructional configurations.

What does the future hold for instructors and the competencies needed to effectively engage in the fields of teaching and learning? How long will this set of instructor competencies remain viable? At best, we can purport that the 2021 instructor competencies reflect what is current but what is also stable enough to be relevant and adaptable going forward. The following underlying assertions support this set of instructor competencies and as such, the foundation for this set of instructor competencies is solidly supported from research and practice.

TABLE 9.1 Comparison of Updated Instructor Competencies to 2004 Statements

2004 Competencies	Updated 2021 Competencies
5 Domains and 18 Competencies	**4 Domains and 19 Competencies**
Professional Foundations • Communicate effectively • Update and improve one's professional knowledge and skills • Comply with established ethical and legal standards • Establish and maintain professional credibility	*Professional Foundations* • Effective communication • Improvement of instructor practices • Anticipation of situational factors • Ethical and legal standards • Establishment of professionalism • Management of instructional resources
Planning and Preparation • Plan instructional methods and materials • Prepare for instruction	*Designing for Learning* • Specification of expected learning • Plan instructional approach • Plan instructional resources • Preparation of instructional/learning activities • Preparation of assessment and feedback
Instructional Methods and Strategies • Stimulate and sustain learner motivation and engagement • Demonstrate effective presentation skills • Demonstrate effective facilitation skills • Demonstrate effective questioning skills • Provide clarification and feedback • Promote retention of knowledge and skills • Promote transfer of knowledge and skills • Use media and technology to enhance learning and performance	*Facilitating Learning* • Learner engagement • Instruction adaptation to learners/learning environment • Learning promotion through feedback • Retention and promotion of knowledge, skills, and attitudes • Transfer of learned knowledge, skills, and attitudes to other contexts • Application of class management principles
Assessment and Evaluation • Assess learning and performance • Evaluate instructional effectiveness	*Evaluating Learning* • Plan and preparation for monitoring and evaluating instruction • Evaluation of instructional effectives
Management • Manage an environment that fosters learning and performance • Manage the instructional process through the appropriate use of technology	∅

Assertion 1

The goal of instruction is to facilitate learning and improve performance. In instructional settings, learning is a two-way street, in that instructors and students are both learning. The competencies and standards within this book are intended to demonstrate the knowledge, skills, attitudes, and growth identity needed to effectively perform the job tasks and roles of an instructor. We encourage instructors to use the competencies outlined in their professional practice to support their organizations and learners to meet instructional and organizational objectives.

Assertion 2

The 2021 IBSTPI instructor competencies and standards are applicable to a wide array of professional contexts (e.g., military, corporate, higher education, etc.), instructional settings (i.e., face-to-face, online, and blended), and instructional approaches (e.g., lecture, discussion, small group activities, etc.). IBSTPI conducted rigorous research based on current conceptions of instructors and validated these competencies and standards using a sample from across international borders. The competencies are intended to extend across professional contexts and international contexts that are both formal (e.g., school) and informal (e.g., workplace) learning environments.

Assertion 3

Instructors, irrespective of their job title, are responsible for a broad range of KSAs that involve planning, delivering, and evaluating instructional processes and activities intended to facilitate learning and improve performance. The 2021 IBSTPI competencies are conducive to individuals who facilitate learning and improve performance within their job tasks. Furthermore, the role of an instructor may vary in job titles across cultures, organizations, and professional contexts (e.g., teacher, facilitator, trainer, professor, etc.).

Assertion 4

The 2021 IBSTPI instructor competencies are agnostic towards the selection and deployment of specific vendor technologies for designing, facilitating, and evaluating the instructional program or product as the current draft of the performance statements and competencies are applicable to any instructional setting (i.e., core, online, and blended) irrespective of the specific technologies used to support the job activities of the instructor.

Assertion 5

Contextual factors such as the instructional setting (i.e., core, blended, and online), the professional context (e.g., military, corporate, higher education, etc.), regulations, policies, and practices (e.g., FERPA, HIPAA, etc.), and local culture can influence the extent to which the 2021 IBSTPI instructor competencies and performance statements are affected. While the 2021 IBSTPI competencies and performances are intended to generalize, instructors will inevitably "tailor" the competencies and standards to the unique requirements of their context.

The 2021 IBSTPI instructor competencies are a snapshot in time of the evolving role of instructors in a range of professional contexts (e.g., K–12, higher education, workplace, etc.). Our hope is that the 2021 IBSTPI instructor competencies will assist both researchers and practitioners in the next decade as they create, facilitate, and evaluate instructional and learning experiences in the emerging settings in which instructors perform for their organizations. Future iterations of instructor competencies may reflect different domains which will account for the newer technologies, environments, and pedagogies that will emerge to meet learner needs. As we finish writing this book, the emergence of artificial intelligence (AI) tools such as ChatGPT and the impact AI has on teaching and learning are beginning to be an important topic of discussion among those who instruct. We hope the next iteration of instructor competencies will take a deeper look into the impact AI and other emerging technologies have on instructor competencies.

REFERENCES

Frondozo, C. E., King, R. B., Nalipay, M. J. N., & Mordeno, I. G. (2020). Mindsets matter for teachers, too: Growth mindset about teaching ability predicts teachers' enjoyment and engagement. *Current Psychology, 41*, 5030–5033. https://doi.org/10.1007/s12144-020-01008-4

Körkkö, M., Kyrö-Ämmälä, O., & Turunen, T. (2016). Professional development through reflection in teacher education. *Teaching and Teacher Education, 55*, 198–206. https://doi.org/10.1016/j.tate.2016.01.014

Yeager, D. S., Carroll, J. M., Buontempo, J., Cimpian, A., Woody, S., Crosnoe, R., & Dweck, C. S. (2022). Teacher mindsets help explain where a growth-mindset intervention does and doesn't work. *Psychological Science, 33*(1), 18–32. https://doi.org/10.1177/09567976211028984

Yeager, D. S., & Dweck, C. S. (2020). What can be learned from growth mindset controversies? *American Psychologist, 75*(9), 1269–1284. https://doi.org/10.1037/amp0000794

Zeichner, K. M., & Liston, D. P. (2013). *Reflective teaching: An introduction.* Routledge.